Kids Don't Bat Rocks Anymore

Dennie Bridges

To my mother Maxine Bridges.

About a month before she died I gave her a

manuscript to read for an "unbiased" critique.

Would you believe, she thought it was "wonderful."

Acknowledgments

I owe a special thanks to a number of people for their help. To my son Steve Bridges and to Ed Alsene for help in editing and to Bill Colburn for sharing memories. Thanks also Gary Schwartz for his talented formatting.

Thanks also to the Michael J. Fox Foundation. As I was "running" the channels one evening I landed on Michael being interviewed on the Screen Actor's Studio. I was so impressed with his determination and commitment to finding a cure for Parkinson's that I contacted his foundation with an offer to donate all my book profits to help find a cure. Special gifts officer Amanda McDorman and the Fox Foundation have been supportive at every turn.

Forward

We met in the fall of 1957. We were away from home for the first time having both enrolled at Illinois Wesleyan University. Little did we suspect that we would become best friends, would watch and worry about one another's families, would travel with our wives throughout the world and would spend endless hours in "spirited" political discussions. Neither did we suspect, especially having witnessed each other's undergraduate performance, that we would end up devoting our lives to higher education.

But fate has its way, and now, almost fifty years later, we can look back over our lives grateful for the good times we have shared and the wonderful careers we have had.

In retrospect, it should not be surprising that Dennie and I became best friends and that our lives unfolded in similar ways. We were both products of small rural communities tucked into a unique time and place in the history of our nation. When we talk today there is no need to spend time building "common ground." In fact, from the very first day, there was no need for us to establish who we were or what we held as shared values.

This book is a glimpse of the world we shared as we grew up in the middle of the twentieth century, in the middle of the country, and in the middle of Illinois. We lived in different yet similar communities about forty or fifty miles apart, but our experiences were much the same. This book captures those experiences and records them not only for the sake of restoring the memory of times past but also for providing a look at the values developed by life in these small farm towns.

For those who lived in a small rural community in the 1940's and 1950' this book will trigger memories. As you read you will probably have stories of your own to add to ones that Dennie has recorded, but for those who did not grow up in these times or in a small farm town, the stories told in the pages of this book will provide you with a view of a social setting that you may not have known existed. Stories of communities where everyone knew one another and, more importantly, cared about one another. Stories of games and competitive events often times simply concocted by youngsters who had no organized parks and recreation schedule to follow. Stories of pranks and creative mischief that were a major part of small town life, and stories of love and concern for neighbors that played out in simple acts of kindness to one another. Beyond giving the reader a light and humorous look at life gone by this book provides support for an idea that is important for all to consider. As William Shakespeare noted in *King Henry IV*, "There is a history in all men's lives." In this book, the reader comes face to face with the simple truth that we all come from some place and that place is important in determining who we are and what we believe. For two college roommates who have enjoyed a lifetime of friendship and decades of shared good times these lessons are clear. May this book give others cause to reflect on their history and the impact it had on their lives. Luke, the featured character in the book might be Dennie, he might be me, or if you were from a small town he might be you.

C. WILLAM COLBURN, Ph.D
Emeritus Professor
University of Michigan

Prologue

In the last half-century or so, there has been a dramatic movement from small towns to larger cities. There are many reasons for this movement—technology and centralization of jobs and markets and a variety of cultural and economic changes to name a few. There have been many pluses and minuses socially. One significant outcome of this migration is that small towns like the one in this story have mostly not grown or have even gotten smaller as the activities in these places have moved to bigger cities. Young people growing up in either type of location are impacted. In the larger towns, there are often more opportunities but kids can get lost in the shuffle and a sense of close-knit community is difficult to find. In the small towns that remain, school consolidation and loss of people and businesses to the bigger cities have diminished community feeling, and perhaps left lesser prospects for success.

Today, life seems to be racing at kids at a thousand miles an hour. Television and cell phones, the Internet and video games, fast food, instant news and multi-tasking are all part of an "on-the-go" culture. Children have crammed schedules, every activity or event is structured, and hauling kids to and from organized activities is all-consuming for parents.

There once was a different way— the life of a farm town kid in the 1950's and earlier—and that is what this book is about. It's about a kid that I've named Luke and his family and his friends and his small town. Some of the stories are about special experiences and some just everyday happenings. Whether Luke was typical or average is unclear. The stories are true, most of them from Luke's memory. Searching Luke's memory was a little bit of a mysterious adventure because there was no blueprint for what he could remember.

Luke's town was not Mayberry. There were no Barney Fifes, (although there were a few "Aunt Beas") and not everything turned out all right at the end of each day. It was a hard working farm community with few outside influences on young people. Most kids didn't have a lot of fancy toys and they made up or organized most games on their own, making up rules as they went along. Some games had to be altered to fit the smaller number of players. Kids probably grew up a bit naïve and in some cases blissfully ignorant, but they also may have been a bit more creative and trusting. Most knew something about hard work.

This isn't a nostalgia trip down memory lane where everything then was wonderful. There were many things from that time that weren't so good. And there are some things that, sadly, are not so good today. Whether growing up in a small farming community 50 or 60 years ago was better than growing up today in a suburb or big city is a personal call. I know many kids today would not be turned on by "the good old days" and most people are comfortable with what they know. On the other hand, there are some lessons to be learned from the simplicity of small town life and some kids just might go for it if they had a chance to find out what it is really like.

Telling Luke's story is a little fuzzy because it happened a long time ago. The ability to look through a lens changed by time and perspective provides the opportunity to add some thoughts on Luke and the town and how things have changed and in some cases stayed the same.

Chapter 1

Knowing a little bit about the town Luke lived in is a good place to begin.

Route 165, possibly the shortest state route in Illinois, ran by the north side of Luke's town. It is a concrete highway and was then always referred to as the "hard road." In those days, most of the country roads were gravel and a few were dirt. When the weather was bad people in town would often hear the warning that they had better take the "hard road," or, be careful of the traffic on the hard road. It was a little bit like being sure to put the milk in the "ice box." Even after the invention of the electric refrigerator Luke's family couldn't seem to get away from calling it the "ice box."

There was also the constant warning to stay off the "Belt Line," which was a four-lane highway around Bloomington, the biggest city in the area. The son of the founder of Luke's town was killed when he was a young man in a grisly decapitation accident at a Belt Line intersection. This accident made par-

2

ents and other townspeople so wary they would say, "stay off the Belt Line, they drive like mad men on that highway."

Luke's town was much like many other towns in America, but he and his friends thought it was kind of special. Many towns designate themselves as the "World Capitol" of something or other. There is one town in Illinois that proclaims itself the "Pig Capitol of the World" and there was a guy who got a kick out of telling his buddies that that was where his wife was from! Luke's town, though, was not really the capitol of anything.

The only street in Luke's town that had a name was Main Street and even then there was no street sign. It was just very clearly the "Main" street in town. There were two streets running parallel to Main Street on both the north and south with three short cross streets creating three Main Street corners. At the extreme west end of town was the school and the ball diamonds. At the east end of town was the business district. Main Street was a little over a half mile long and ran east to west. The railroad track ran diagonally through town, actually cutting off a small southeast section of the town.

Luke lived in this section. In some towns when you go to the business district you "go uptown," or in others you go "downtown," Luke's family went "over to town."

Luke lived next door to the telephone office. All calls had to go through the switchboard at the telephone office, which was just a room in Luke's next-door neighbor's home. Manning the switchboard was a 24 hour job. Someone had to be available at all hours every day. There was a cot in the switchboard room where someone slept to handle calls that were made in the wee hours of the morning.

Most people, particularly the farmers were on a party line. Seven or eight homes would be on the same line. Two long rings and a short might be Farmer Jones, while three short rings and a long might be Farmer Smith. It was common for someone to be on a call and hear the click of other phones coming off the hook. People didn't share a lot of personal information on a party line. Some friends on the same party line would have a pre-arranged time, say Sunday evening at 7 o'clock, when they would just pick up the phone and visit. There were no ringing phones to alert others that anyone was using the telephone line.

Luke's family had a private line. It was the shortest line in town (about 50 feet), stretching across the small lawn to the house next door. Even a private line wasn't totally private. The operator could listen in on any call. The telephone was important in taking fuel and gas orders for Luke's dad. Often when the whole family would leave home, they would ask the operator to answer their calls and take orders.

In an emergency, the operator could make all of the party lines ring continuously. It was ring, ring, ring, ring, ring, ring— there is a barn fire on at Jimmy Hall's farm —ring, ring, ring,

Northeast Main St. corner

ring, ring, ring, ring, ring, there is a barn fire at Jimmy Hall's farm. This was an early version of the 911 system.

There was a lot of commerce in town and the business district could have been described as thriving. The traffic of pick-up trucks and farm machinery as well as automobiles was heavy and finding a parking space was not always easy. The major employer in town was a gear company that had many workers. The company manufactured and distributed various farm implements with the premier product being a nine-speed gear mechanism for tractors that one of the owners had invented.

There were two grain elevators that used the railroad to ship grain to the Mississippi River barges. One of the elevators doubled as a lumber yard and was across the street from Luke's home. The noise of the huge corn dryers was often a nighttime irritant.

The town had two car dealers; a Chrysler-Plymouth dealer and a Kaiser-Fraser dealer. Both dealerships had automotive repair shops and there was a constant flow of auto and farm implement repair. It was not uncommon for the mechanics to allow the work to spill over into the street. Repairing or replacing a tractor tire took up a lot of space, so traffic just had to maneuver around the workplace.

There was a busy blacksmith shop on the south side of town. The shop had a forge and the blacksmith often did horse-shoe-

Southwest Main St. corner

ing work. It seemed as if farm machinery had a way of breaking down frequently, so the blacksmith was important in getting the farmers back into the fields.

At one time there were two grocery stores, a bank, and a corner tavern. The sidewalk and the bench outside the tavern was the morning gathering place for farmers, particularly if the fields were wet. Diagonally across the corner from the tavern was the United Brethren church. This was a strategic location for the church. There were a few men who would drop their wives off for a church function and wait for them in the bar.

(The Church of England built churches at the edge of towns with the vicarage next door. The next building was most often the pub. This was for the pleasure and convenience of the pastor and his flock. Luke doesn't remember his pastor spending any time at the bar.)

At one time, before the gear company moved in, on the second floor of a vacant building there was sort of a rundown pool hall. No one seemed to know exactly what went on up there but a card game of some sort was whispered about. Luke and his friends snuck up there once and it was kind of a grungy place. Anyone in town looking for a real pool hall had to go to a slightly larger town about four miles down the road that had two. In one of them there was a sign in the restroom that said, "Please flush the toilet, Lexington needs the drinking water." (Lexington being a neighboring town and a big sports rival.)

At the north edge of the business district was an egg distribution plant. Eggs were trucked in from a large area to be sorted, graded and distributed to wholesalers. They had an egg-candling operation which employed a few women in Luke's town. These ladies would work in a dark room and candle eggs, scanning the eggs with a strong light looking for blood spots. The egg industry says that blood spots do not make eggs dangerous, but they remove any eggs that have them. (Blood spots do not sound good!)

The big joke told at the egg plant was that a guy is eating at a diner and the waitress says "we now have calves tongue, would you like to try some?" The guy says, "God no, I could never eat something that came out of a cow's mouth!" "Gimme some eggs."

The tiny post office was next door to the egg distributorship. There was no home delivery of mail, so there was a wall of small mail boxes with combination locks where townspeople came to get their mail. They could buy a three-cent stamp for a letter, or save a little money and send a penny post card.

The federal post office inspectors would have frowned on the Postmaster allowing Luke space on the mail sorting table to unwrap and count the newspapers that he delivered each morning. The mail room was tiny and part of what was good about small towns was helping each other out.

Chapter One

There was no police station or police officers nor did the town have a fire department. Crime was virtually nonexistent. Very few families ever locked their homes, even when they went out of town. Only once did a house burn down.

There was no garbage pick-up so everyone had backyard trash burners.

Almost all of the alleys in town were grass and the home-owners mowed the alleys as if they were an extension of their yards. A few people raised chickens in town and they liked for people to collect their lawn clippings and "pitch" them into the chicken yard so that the chickens could feed on the insects.

The most striking visual feature of the town were the rows of black walnut trees flanking the three half-mile roads leading into town and along all of the city streets. These were planted by the town's founder in 1899.

There was occasional talk about cutting down the trees that grew along the grain fields. The shade of the trees negatively affected the crop yield of the first few rows of beans or corn but the family that farmed the land were descendants of the town's founder and couldn't bring themselves to destroy their forefather's handiwork.

The presence of the trees resulted in a huge squirrel population—there were probably more squirrels in town than people. The human population in 1955 was 140, with 15 of these under 18 years old. The age breakdown for the squirrels was unavailable.

There was some squirrel hunting and the meat was used for a squirrel stew. Squirrel meat has been described as "stringy." Stringy and meat in the same sentence never sounded real good.

Across the street from the business district was a wooded park with a few picnic tables.

Social highlights of each summer included the twice monthly free movies. The kids never really dwelled on who paid the "movie man," but every other Wednesday night they would stretch a white sheet between two trees and play a movie. It was a big event for the tavern and grocery store and there were outdoor popcorn and candy vendors as well.

There weren't any first-run movies, instead there were a lot of shoot'em up westerns. The projector would break down at least once every showing. There were occasions when the movies would be canceled in advance because of rain, but if it started raining during the movie they just pressed on and people either used an umbrella or headed for a strategically parked car.

The adults brought their lawn chairs and the kids usually spread out blankets. There was the occasional pee shooter or water pistol incident, but for the most part it was a fun night at the movies.

Leading up to show time, there was some dead time to fill, often kids just "hanging out."

There was a kid in town who was a bed-wetter. He was taking pills to try to cure the condition and the pills made the color of his urine a bright blue. Luke remembers that before the free show one night, without revealing his bed wetting problem, this kid bragged that he could "pee blue." He charged some guys a dime each and went out behind the grain elevator and put on a bright blue pissing exhibition. It was a real stretch sometimes for quality entertainment, this had to be described as an "added attraction."

The morning after the free show, it was a race between the town kids and the store owner to get to the park first to pick up the empty bottles. The deposit on each bottle was two cents. The store owner was a little testy when the kids would get there first and then return the bottles to his store for the deposit pay-off.

One final area of note was an old abandoned coal mine at the south edge of the town. The mine was never really that productive and was shut down sometime before 1920. Luke and his friends were always warned about how dangerous it was to play at the mine site because there was only a rickety barbed wire fence around the main mine shaft. The kids used to play "guns" there, using the brick ruins of buildings for cover. There were a number of half walls and some partial chimneys, which made good hiding places.

There were scores of wild rabbits around the ruins which the kids would chase on a regular basis. On one occasion while trying to get away a rabbit got wedged into a narrow space between two brick walls. The kids could reach in and barely touch the rabbit's fur, but not far enough to capture it.

They really had no plan for what to do with it if they caught it. But it was the thrill of the hunt, just something to do. The capture plan was to use a long wooden pole as a battering ram and chip away at the bricks until they could reach the rabbit. At one point Luke put his thumb up against the brick and said "give it a shot right here." His buddies did just that, not waiting for him to pull back his thumb.

Luke's THUMB was blackened and was throbbing like in a cartoon. This was really a smart bunch he was running with.

The site is now a cornfield with no sign of any kind that it once was a coal mine. If that main mine shaft was so deep and so dangerous, it's a wonder they were ever able to fill it up. Someday a corn harvesting combine may drive over that spot at harvest time and disappear.

So this was Luke's town, surrounded on four sides by farm fields. Acres and acres of corn, or beans, or alfalfa. This is where he grew up; where he played, worked, went to school and developed an outlook on life.

Chapter 2

Growing up in a small town in the late 1940's and early 1950's was a mixed bag of experiences. In a lot of ways Luke was sheltered from what went on in the world. He read only the sports pages of the newspaper. He knew that wars were being fought and he was aware of the attack on Pearl Harbor, but had no idea where it was, and he knew very little of the political ramifications, foreign or domestic. When he was very young, there were no television newscasts. Once in a while at the theatre he would get to see a PATHE' newsreel of world events.

A very important issue and widely discussed topic in today's world is diversity. Luke's community was entirely Caucasian with diversity being hog farmer, cattle farmer or grain farmer.

The religious persuasion of the community was over-whelmingly Protestant Christian. There were a few Catholics and many Catholic mothers were wary of their children dating non-Catholics. There were no Jews or Muslims and probably no atheists. Like most small farming towns it was very homogeneous.

Years later, as a freshman in college, a Jewish classmate engaged Luke in a conversation about his views on anti-Semitism. He wanted to know how Luke felt about Jewish people. Luke said that he honestly didn't have an answer. He didn't know if he had ever met a Jewish person. He didn't think he knew anything about the Holocaust. He said that he had heard the phrase "did you Jew him down," but really never tied it to any kind of prejudice.

Luke was also a college freshman when he had his first conversation with African Americans. There were two black players on his football team. People in his small community had only rare opportunities to be around "Negroes." It was a big deal when the Harlem Globetrotters played a game at the local high school gym. People were humming "Sweet Georgia Brown" for weeks and talking happily about Goose Tatum and Marques Haynes. There was a black man living in Bellflower, a neighboring town, who was a referee. All of the fans felt that he was absolutely the best basketball referee in the area and they enjoyed talking with him at games. It is possible that the uniqueness of him being virtually the only black living in any of these rural communities had an impact on how he was rated as an official. Was he really that good or was he just different?

Luke knew the value of a hard day's labor, the people in his town worked hard and Luke was no exception. He developed pretty good communications skills by interacting with adults. He needed a lot of work on social graces, but he had a solid church-going foundation.

The fact that his small town was in an agricultural area was a factor in his growing up as was the fact that his dad's occupation was driving a gas truck. His family never had much money which was a factor in his learning some frugality, but he never felt deprived. By the time he was in high school he could drive his dad's big tanker truck and deliver gas and other fuels and he knew enough to get each in the proper tank.

Sports was a passion in his family which brought Luke lots of happiness and excitement. He could name almost all of the major league baseball players and their statistics. He could throw a football, hit a fastball and shoot a long set shot.

The fact that this happened about a half-century ago was a huge factor, the information highway then was pretty much a dirt road. A picture taken during this time period was in black and white and it helped to "lick" the end of the flash-bulb before plugging it into the camera.

One thing that made an early impact on Luke was our nation's involvement in war.

There was a canning factory in Gibson City, a city about ten miles from Luke's little town where German prisoners of war were held in a work camp. These prisoners were brought to his family's house on the edge of town to get a drink of water. They were at work pulling weeds out of a bean field across the street from where his family lived. He must have been only about five years old, but he was big enough to be the one to hand-pump the water from the well. It was not widely known then or now that German POW's were shipped to camps in America.

Luke's eyes were pretty much glued to the machine guns that the two guards held casually as the German soldiers drank thirstily. He thought that the Germans looked like giants.

In Luke's small town and the surrounding farm community there seemed to be a more visceral reaction to the war in the Pacific with Japan than to the war in Europe with Germany. As a kid, Luke heard lots of references to the "yellow Japs" and doesn't remember hearing derogatory comments about the "Krauts."

A national perspective would have been that in Europe we were coming to the aid of the Allies in fighting Germany, while the Japanese intentionally attacked the United States at Pearl Harbor.

Locally, the farming community was heavily German Lutheran, which may have tempered the hate for the German people somewhat, while race I'm sure was a factor in hating the Japanese.

Except for his family flattening tin cans and saving them for the war effort, Luke was too young to really be aware of World

War II, and it was an eye opener to have the enemy soldiers in his back yard.

Luke and his family also experienced air raid warnings, though he was very young. The town siren sounded to warn everyone in town to douse their lights. Luke would go with his mom and sister and lay on their bed until the all-clear sounded. No one thought that German or Japanese aircraft were flying over the town. It was just a practice drill.

Later, on VJ day, Luke's family was in the city at a Steak-n'-Shake drive-in when the news of the armistice in Japan was broadcast on the radio. A sailor in the next car jumped onto his car roof and danced. The war in the Pacific was over.

Even later, in the mid-fifties, when the news reached his town that the North Koreans had crossed the 38th parallel, he didn't really know where to look for Korea on the map. It was sad to think that the country was back at war again.

Chapter 3

The town's schoolhouse was a two story stucco building with two big class rooms on the first floor and three classrooms and a music room on the second floor.

When Luke was in the first grade, there were four grades in his room taught by one teacher.

There were a total of 14 students in the room—five in the first grade, two in the second grade, four in the third grade and three in the fourth grade. Four of the kids lived in town and the rest were from farm families.

The fifth, sixth, seventh and eighth grades were in the other downstairs classroom and the high school was upstairs.

There were five boys near Luke' age in town and their families' activities were somewhat interwoven because of their kids' activities. The occupations of the fathers were varied; a hardware store owner, a basketball coach, a school principal, a grain elevator and gear company owner and a gas truck operator who sold petroleum products to the farmers. There

19

were also two girls his age living in town and there were some younger sisters and brothers.

As kids, no one was taught to call the other's parents "Mr. and Mrs." The first names were George and Stella, Coach and Marian, Ted and Margaret, Elmo and LaVerne and Dudley and Maxine. The coach's first name was Paul, but the kids all called him Coach.

Luke's very first day in school he was in trouble and was summoned to the principal's office. The kids were all sitting at their desks when the principal's secretary knocked on the door and told the teacher that Luke was to go with her to the principal's office.

The principal, Mr. Abell, said that when Luke had passed him in the hallway he had said, "Hi, Ted." He told Luke that now he was in school that he would have to call him "Mr. Abell." Luke asked him, "What about Margaret, can I still call Mrs. Abell Margaret?" The principal assured Luke that he could continue to call his wife Margaret.

At a neighboring small town there were brothers who were in the second and third grade who had attended a one room school house. When they moved to a slightly bigger school in town, riding the bus to school was a new and scary experience. On the first day of school they were afraid that they wouldn't get on the right bus after school. The third grader consoled his brother and told him not to worry. "Just remember that our bus is the yellow one!" he advised.

There was a farm boy in the third grade who wore the same badly worn cloth bib overalls to school every day. They were really floods, and one pant leg was a lot shorter than the other. They were a faded grayish blue and one of the shoulder straps was always pinned with a safety pin. Who knows how often they were washed, but he wore them every day over a long-sleeved work shirt. One day after Christmas he came to school wearing a brand new pair of Oshkosh denim bibs. All of the kids in the room congratulated him and patted him on the back. You would have thought that he had made a game-winning hoop. The Oshkosh pair then became his everyday outfit. They could only hope that he burned the cloth pair?

In fourth grade geography Luke's class studied the continent of Africa. They were surprised to discover that there were not, in fact, any tigers in Africa. They are found in India, Malaysia, China and of course Detroit (Detroit Tigers!), but not in Africa.

At breakfast one morning Luke was eating a bowl of Kellogg's Rice Krispies or Corn Flakes. On the back of the cereal carton was a display of the "wild animals of Africa", and sure enough, there was a picture of a tiger. Luke couldn't wait to get to school to show the box to his teacher and tell her that she was wrong. There were indeed tigers in Africa. It said so right on the back of the cereal box.

Luke's teacher was a feisty little lady and she let him known in no uncertain terms that she wasn't wrong, the Kellogg company was wrong.

The class decided that Luke should spearhead a protest to Kelloggs by writing a letter to the Battle Creek, Michigan company to point out the tiger error. It was David vs Goliath, as this fourth grade class was one of the earliest consumer watchdogs.

Can you visualize the response of the Production Manager of the Kellogg Company?

"Let me get this straight, some fourth grade student from Podunk grade school says we are wrong to include a tiger in our animals from Africa display on our cereal box? He says that there are no tigers in Africa? And he is right?"

The class received a reply from Kellogg admitting the error and indicating that at the start of the next production run they would correct the mistake. Luke's class was thrilled! Their teacher's African data was validated and Luke was a bit of a hero for paying attention to what he had learned in class. Luke could look back at this as an academic highlight of his life.

At the end of every school year, everyone was excited to get their report card to see if they had passed. One year one of the five town boys passed on the condition that he take a course over the summer at University High School in a near-by city.

Everyone was asking everyone else if they had passed. This kid proudly said, "hell, I not only passed, I passed on condition!" It was like he was getting extra credit.

Luke's school had a small gymnasium. It didn't seem small to them and in the winter they played there before school, at recess, during noon hour and at basketball practice after school. The kids always left a window unlocked so that they could play on week-ends. The gym was so short that it had a double 10-second line, one at each edge of the center circle. The result was that the center circle was in the front court at each end. There were two rows of seats down one side of the court. On the other side of the court there was a stage and a small section of two-row seating. The seating capacity couldn't have been more than 200.

The gym had an electronic scoreboard called a "ShadowGraph" which was invented and patented by an inventor in Luke's small town. This man also was a school bus driver. The scoreboard featured a white number flashed on a gray background. Many of the small town gyms in the area had this scoreboard, but technology soon passed it by and everyone went to numbers that were individual light bulbs. The town's tiny scoreboard business went under.

The scoreboard time clock was a regular clock face of eight minutes and was lit with white lights until the last minute of a quarter when it would turn red, hence the term "the clock is in the red."

The high school team had passed down to the grade school team a set of uniforms.

The jerseys were unique in that the back of the jersey had a flap that went under the crotch and buttoned in front. They were designed to keep shirt tales tucked in the pants. This is a feature that maybe should make a comeback! Luke thought they were neat, but the pants were so tight that on the little guys, the orange shirt was peeking out of the leg holes.

Luke's eighth grade team went undefeated. They beat Cropsey twice, Cooksville twice and Colfax twice to go 6 - 0. A few years earlier Taylorville had become the first team to go unbeaten and win the Illinois High School State Tournament. Luke's grade school coach told everyone that they and Taylorville were the only unbeaten teams in the state's history.

When Luke was playing on the lightweight grade school team, they had a game at LeRoy. Some of the fans sat on a single bench on one side of the court. Luke's mother was assessed a technical foul for yelling at the referee. And people wonder where he got his competitiveness!

Luke's school had the best fire escape anywhere. The building was a pretty tall two story building and the fire escape was an enclosed tube that had a small curve at the top and then a steep slide into a small sand pit. The school kids played more on the fire escape than they did on any of the playground equipment. By using their hands and feet to brace against the sides, they could "crab" walk to the top. Using a piece of wax paper to slide on, they could "fire" out like a torpedo into the sand landing area.

Away from school, if they weren't playing some sport, the boys often played "guns." They all had a couple of toy pistols and one kid in town had an arsenal of toy weapons. They would split into teams and one team would hide in a building and the other would go find them. If someone really "got the drop" on a guy – "it was bang, bang your dead." Some guys, though, simply would never admit they were hit and go down. This caused many game-ending arguments.

At one point they all decided to legitimatize the game to a degree and went home to get their air rifle BB guns. They went to one kid's grandma's house and got some of her "old lady" heavy stockings. They cut eye-holes in the hose and pulled them over their heads for some protection and they all wore long sleeved shirts and gloves. They had a rule against shooting at anyone's head. This was going to put an end to any doubt as to who was and was not shot. One of the mothers got wind of the plan and put the kibosh on it.

The only gun Luke ever owned was a BB gun. He would go sparrow hunting some, but he very rarely hit a bird. There was a Korean war vet that walked around the neighborhood with a 22 gauge rifle shooting starlings and sparrows. He was so good that nine or ten cats followed him around.

Luke never shot a shotgun. Many of his friends went rabbit and pheasant hunting. While they were walking in wintry weather over broken corn stalks looking to shoot game Luke was in the warm gymnasium shooting basketballs. He didn't want to kill rabbits or pheasants and he certainly didn't want to clean them after they were dead. Back then game was plentiful and Luke respected how much some of his friends enjoyed hunting. Most were responsible, although a couple of guys used a spotlight and hunted at night out of the backseat of their car. This probably made them ineligible for the outdoor sportsman of the year award!

One of Luke's friends tried to interest him in fur trapping. This friend had a line of traps on the Mackinaw River, and he was mostly trying to catch muskrats. Luke agreed to get up at daybreak before school and "walk" the trap lines with him. It was dark and cold and the snow was deep. There was only one trap sprung and in it was a muskrat leg. There was evidence to indicate that the muskrat had chewed his own leg off to escape. Think about that for a minute! A skinned and stretched pelt was not that valuable.

One day of this was more than enough for Luke, Davy Crockett he was not.

Luke did walk the cornfields after harvest at times. Back then the corn pickers left lots of ears of corn in the field. If the farmer had cattle and the field was fenced in, he would turn the cattle loose in the field to graze on the corn that the picker missed. Farmers who didn't have fences would often allow school groups to pick up the corn as a fund-raising project. The band did this at Luke's school.

The farmer would fasten a wooden divider in the center of a corn wagon so that students could walk along either side of the wagon, pick up ears of corn and hurl them into the wagon. The divider was a backboard to bank high tosses off. Sometimes an errant throw over the top would be mistaken as intentional and there would be a quick flurry of "corn wars." It was all in good fun—and the band could buy new uniforms.

Before high school age, there were very few organized sports activities, and since there were only four other boys in town Luke's age he often had to invent sports games to play alone or he and his friends alter the rules of games to fit the lesser numbers.

Luke's big standby was batting rocks. His family had a gravel driveway that led from the alley to their garage. At one time there were lots of rocks in the gravel (Before Luke batted them all out). When the men's team would break a bat on Sunday, as batboy, Luke would claim the bat and take it home for repair. If it was just cracked, a couple of small finishing nails and a little tape made it usable. Luke had many broken bats. His three favorites were a Joe DiMaggio model, a Rocky Colavito model and a Johnny Mize model.

The game rules were pretty simple. Luke hit across his garden and the neighbor's garden, aiming at the outfield wall which was the neighbor's old barn. This barn had lightening rods at each end, which Luke used as foul poles. A rock hit over the barn between the foul poles was a home run, a rock hitting the roof was a base hit and anything else was an out. Luke would switch hit a lot, throwing a rock in the air with his right hand while batting left-handed and throwing a rock in the air with his left hand when batting right-handed. He kept track of his batting average and home run totals for every 480 at-bats, which was at that time the major league minimum to qualify for the batting title. He would try to have sessions of a minimum 100 at-bats. He was, of course, trying to hit more than 60 homers and break Babe Ruth's record.

Luke got a little math work in by dividing his hits by his at-bats to come up with his batting average.

The bats didn't last too long. After hitting a couple hundred rocks the barrel of the bat looked like a dog had been chewing on it. There was an endless supply of bats, as three or four would be cracked every Sunday. The man living next door lived alone and was not home a lot. He mentioned to Luke a couple of times how his wooden shingle roof was being damaged (it was really old and decrepit to start with). So after a while Luke had to schedule his rock batting for times when the neighbor wasn't home and carefully watch for his car coming down the street, which temporarily suspended the game.

The blacktop leading into town was just on the "home run" side of the shed. Luke tried to avoid hitting when a car was coming, but nicked a couple of hub caps as he was screaming and begging for the rock to get down! "Get down!"

Luke also created games with a rubber baseball. He and his family lived near a lumber yard which had a garage with a slanted roof. The garage was located across a gravel drive from some metal grain bins. The object of the game was to set up chances to make leaping outfield catches against the grain bin wall. Luke would stand really close to the garage and throw the ball high in the air aiming to land it on the slanted roof and then race to the wall to try to make a Mickey Mantle catch against the grain bin. The difficulty of the catch depended on the height of the throw and exactly where the ball hit the roof. Some catches were routine and some impossible, but once in a while Luke was able to make that scintillating major league catch. He got knocked on his butt a fair amount but refused to be "wall shy" and often verbally narrated the action: "Back, back, back, he makes the catch!"

Luke drew a strike zone on the back of another neighbor's shed. He would pretend he was a pitcher trying to throw a perfect game. Every pitch had to be somewhere in the strike zone with his rubber baseball and every ricocheting ground ball had to be fielded cleanly.

Chapter Three

Twenty-seven straight (nine innings, three outs) was a perfect game. One miss was a one-hitter, two misses a two-hitter, four hits a loss. Luke was very goal-oriented.

There was no Little League baseball anywhere in the area, so the kids played a lot of pick- up games. They played three on two unless one of the farm kids could get to town or they could talk Luke's sister and her friend (the two girls in town) to play.

The games were definitely high scoring. A team might be behind 15 - 0, but still have a chance to win because they hadn't even batted yet. A ball hit to right field was an automatic out, except when the one left-handed hitter batted, and then a ball hit to left field was out. They would also play pitcher's hands were out so that a team didn't have to have a first baseman. If someone fielded a ground ball and threw the ball to the pitcher before the runner made it to first, the batter was out. Do any kids today play or understand "pitcher's hands are out?"

They played a lot of softball at Luke's school. The afternoon recess at the grade school sometimes lasted all afternoon. The kids would go out to play and the male teacher would often go down to flirt with the first grade teacher and call everyone in just in time for the country kids to catch the bus. The girls and boys often played softball together to have enough kids to make two teams When they would choose sides, almost always five girls would be among the first 10 picked. On occasion Luke would pick Karen first because she was his girl

Part of the gender tainted team Sibley refused to play.

friend. Luke's sister Kay, Karen, Dorothy, Janet and another Kay were all good hitters. They could run and none of them "threw like a girl."

Do kids now have any feel for choosing up sides? The two people who were the choosers, usually two of the better players, would decide who got to choose first by throwing up a bat. One would toss a bat in the air and the other would catch it in one fist. They would then take turns putting fist on top of fist until someone covered the knob of the bat, which earned him first pick.

31

Chapter Three

At some point when Luke was in the seventh grade he rec-
ognized that a kid named Dempster was always the last kid
chosen. As competitive as Luke was, for some reason this really bothered him a lot. From that point on, when he was choosing he made sure not to let that happen. One day he chose
Dempster first and he remembers how good it made
Dempster feel. It made Luke feel good, too!

They also played "work-up" sometimes before school started
in the morning when there wasn't time for a team game. There
were four batters. Then a catcher, pitcher, first baseman, second baseman, shortstop, third baseman, and then everyone else
scattered in the outfield. When someone arrived and joined
the game he found out who the last outfielder was to establish
his position in "working up." If a batter made a routine out, he
went to the end of the work up order. The catcher became a
batter, the pitcher became catcher, the first baseman became
the pitcher, etc. If the batter flied or lined out, the fielder who
caught the ball traded spots with the batter.

Do kids still know how to organize a game of work-up?

They were decades away from summer travel teams, but on
their own the town kids bought baseball uniforms and lined up
a game with some boys from the neighboring town of Sibley.
With just the five guys in town and one farm kid, they had to
turn to the girls to fill out the team roster. Sibley somehow got
word of the plans to play girls and cancelled the game.

Sibley evidently had no feel for gender equity or proportionality!

Luke had a friend they called Pinky in the nearest town down the road who was a big Red Sox fan. They would play whiffle ball with Pinky being the Red Sox and Luke the Yankees. They had various ground rules that defined base hits, home runs and outs. Pinky had to post a Red Sox line-up and bat left-handed if Ted Williams was up and right-handed if Bobby Doerr was up. Luke in turn batted right-handed when Hank Baur was up and left-handed when Gene Woodling was up.

There was a hoop on Luke's garage and a pole light so that he and his friends could shoot hoops into the night. The court was gravel and Luke's first basketball was leather with football-like seams.

The raised seams and the gravel surface made for a lot of erratic bounces. It helped on a shot if the shooter could get his hand on the seams (just as a passer needed to do when he threw a spiral with a football) so that the rotation of the ball was balanced.

There were a lot of 3 on 3 games and they played many games of "horse." The old leather ball got pretty scarred up.

Girls had the same motivation as boys to be creative in finding things to do. In the absence of Barbie dolls, Luke's sister and her friend would make dolls out of hollyhocks.

Hollyhocks are flowers shaped like badminton birds that grew mostly in the town's alleys.

The girls would use toothpicks to attach an unopened bud as the doll's head, the flower as the hoop skirt and pieces of vine as the arms. Using the white flower for a bride's gown and the pinks and reds and purples for bridesmaids, they could create an entire wedding party to play with.

For both boys and girls roller skating on the town's sidewalks was an activity that was turned into competition. Kids didn't have shoe skates like you would get at a roller rink, but rather the kind that fastened onto the soles of their shoes. Everyone had a "skate key" that they wore around their neck on a shoestring. They used it to tighten the front of the skate and would use strips of rubber inner tube to wrap around the instep to keep the skate on tight.

They would choose teams and play "ditch-em" at night. If a skater stepped off into the grass and listened, he could locate his opponent by listening for the sounds of the metal skates on the concrete.

There was a slab of sidewalk on a hill that was tilted dangerously because of a tree root growing under it. This called for a "ski jump" type landing and it was a wipe out waiting to happen, especially at night.

After the businesses closed at night kids would play "tin can hockey" on the wider business district sidewalks. All suspicions to the contrary, they did not crack the plate glass window at the bank!

Bicycles were their transportation and involved in much of what they did in town. Luke had the most basic of bikes, a used off brand of some sort. Today kids have 10-speeds or mountain bikes, Luke's was "one speed"— as fast as he could peddle.

A couple of the kids in town had the fancy Schwinn models. They featured a cushion front wheel suspension and a horn. Luke never envied those bikes and in races it still got down to how fast a guy could peddle.

They would split into teams and play ditch-em, which was just a glorified chase around town trying to lose the other guys. They would have "Indy" races around the circular drive in the lumber yard. These races, of course, were usually after Memorial Day when they had listened to the Indy 500 on the radio.

When it rained, the kids would go inside and play with bubble gum baseball cards. Luke spent a lot of nickels and dimes buying Topps bubble gum, often throwing the bubble gum away just hoping to come up with a single card that he didn't have in his collection. He had more than 400 different cards, including the Philadelphia A's Elmer Valo and the Mickey Mantle rookie card.

The kids would shuffle the cards and deal each guy a group of players. The number each guy was dealt sort of depended on how many were playing that day. If a kid got 50 cards, the first thing he did was decide on a major league line-up and team roster of 25 players, the major league roster limit. Then he would use the remaining 25 to create a minor league team. After that each kid became the general manager and tried to arrange trades to improve his team.

Often, Luke would make ridiculous trades to acquire all of the Yankee players. There was a kid who was a Cardinal fan who tried to get all of the Cardinal players. There were no winners or losers, but a lot of time could be spent arguing a trade of Stubby Overmire for Tommy Byrne.

Luke spent alot of time arranging and rearranging those cards, even when alone he would deal out cards to himself and create a team. He has often lamented the decision to give his entire collection to a younger cousin. Actually, he wasn't even a first cousin. His grandmother and Luke's father were half-brother and sister. Luke must have felt that he had outgrown them. When the cousin left home to go to the Army, his mother threw the cards away.

Today they would be worth thousands of dollars.

On Saturday nights everyone went to Colfax, a neighboring small town where they had a real theatre. The feature changed three times a week. There was a Friday/Saturday showing, a Sunday/ Monday showing, and a Tuesday/ Wednesday/Thursday showing. The ticket price was 40 cents

Roy Rogers Riders Club

for an adult and a quarter for kids. If you were too young to have a driver's license, a boy-girl date was to meet a girl at the movie and sit with her and hold her hand.

The aisles in the theatre slanted steeply downhill, of course, and occasionally kids would roll jaw breakers or marbles down the hardwood floor. They made a huge racket on the way down and then rattled noisily as they collided with the metal front of the stage. An usher would come down the aisle with a flashlight looking for the culprits. Unfortunately, the evidence was down by the stage.

The theatre owner would have a Saturday serial that he ran over a period of four or five weeks. For example, he would play one fifth of a Tarzan movie the first week and have a trailer urging the kids to "come back next week to see if Tarzan escapes from the gorilla."

It worked, as kids would let their parents know that they had to be sure to go the next Saturday so they wouldn't miss the next Tarzan episode.

Saturday afternoon was also the time that the theatre would hold a Roy Rogers party. Kids would come dressed up as Roy Rogers or Dale Evans and free tickets would be given to the kids with the best costumes. Roy riding his palomino horse Trigger, along with the help of Gabby Hayes, would catch the bad guys. The Sons of the Pioneers accompanied the western saga with songs like "Cool Water" and "Tumbling Tumbleweed."

When Luke and his friends were very young they would play cowboys and everybody wanted to pretend he was Roy and ride Trigger. Hopalong Cassidy with his horse Topper was okay and so was the Lone Ranger with Silver. Nobody wanted to be Gene Autry with Champion because Gene sang too many songs.

Luke and his friends would tie a short rope around a broom and straddle the broomstick with the straw end of the broom serving as the horse's head. The broom had to be one that had been used for a while so that the "taper" was like the horse's mane. When they dismounted from the broom they had to, of course, tie it up.

If you got to town late you would have to park a block away from downtown. After the movie it was a cheeseburger and shake at Mick's Grill or a chocolate or cherry coke at the corner drugstore. The parents would sit on the benches or the raised edge of the sidewalk and the kids would walk up one side of the business district and down the other. There were small groups of boys and small groups of girls. Many times it was one group following the other. The boys' groups would usually find time to stop in at the hardware store to see if any new Louisville Slugger bats had been stocked.

All of the farmers had a really "scrubbed" look. Their faces were a deep brown with a pure white forehead— a "farmer's tan."

Gibson City, a slightly bigger town 15 miles away had a swimming pool. The kids would often lobby to get one of the parents to take them swimming. There was also a swim program at a lake about 30 miles away. They rode a school bus there to swim and tested the sanity of the bus driver by regularly singing "99 Bottles of Beer on the Wall" all the way to the lake and "John Jacob Jinglehimer Smith" all the way home.

At one point, the swimming activity was cut way back because of the ever present fear of getting polio. One girl in the town did get polio and at one time it was thought that it was spread through swimming. The parents were terrified.

This swimming program might have been the only "organized" sports activity for kids. The sports camps, the Little Leagues, the travel teams, the hours in front of the TV, and the GameBoys were way down the road.

The result was that in their younger days, Luke and his friends had to be creative to fill their days. It was a good thing.

Chapter 4

High school was a big adventure for Luke. There were the positive things like winning sports tournaments, school plays, proms and homecoming dances. Then there were some "off the wall" moments that maybe weren't usual. Were these things happening at big schools? Was this a benefit or drawback of the small school experience? Probably a little of both.

Even though Luke's high school was a consolidation of kids from three little towns, it would still be considered a small school. There were 34 kids in his high school class. Luke never worried about an ACT or SAT test score and was not aware that there was any such thing as a class rank. He was bright enough to get by without studying too much. He doesn't remember doing much homework and athletes never seemed to go academically ineligible. Despite an attitude of only mild interest in the educational part of school, in Luke's view, his best teachers were the toughest ones.

He had a history teacher who had a pretty good temper. When this teacher started to get mad his ears would turn a fiery red and his glasses would slide way down on his nose. Luke had one encounter in this class that says something about being tough and good.

The guy sitting in front of Luke was leaning back on the legs of his chair during the history lecture. Slyly, he thought, Luke reached up with his finger and tipped this guy's chair off balance. The kid's chair fell over and the guy's feet went flying in the air causing a huge commotion and much laughter from the class.

As the fallen kid came to his knees, the history teacher with ears red as a beet, came back and smacked him in the forehead with an open hand. He said something like, "don't screw around in my class...."

Luke was sitting as straight-faced as possible thinking that he was home free when this teacher wheeled around and back handed him on the side of the head and knocked him out of his chair. "Don't think you're getting away with anything!" he said. The teacher walked back to the front of the room and resumed his lecture.

It was swift and sure justice with no thoughts on anybody's part of protesting. Here was an excellent teacher who demanded that kids learn something in his class—and not all of it was history.

The school had two successful coaches and both produced winning teams. Each coach had a different coaching style and players reacted differently. If one coach told his team members to do 20 push-ups, they might do 14. If the other coach told them to do 20 push-ups, they would do 25 just to make sure that the coach knew they had done 20.

Luke felt that he learned more from the guy for whom he did 25. This coach also had a strict curfew during the basketball season. He would call a player's home at curfew time. If a parent answered and said that the player was in bed asleep, he would politely ask to have him awakened and brought to the phone. Once in a while he would call at curfew time and then call again 15 minutes later to see if the player had stopped at home for the curfew call and then gone out again. Either trust was not one of this coach's character traits, or he knew his players very well.

Luke had an English teacher who made the class write a theme a week. She would not accept anything that was not creative. She said that Luke would race into class, borrow a pencil from Sandy, a piece of paper from somebody else and then write an A paper. Luke disputes the charge that he never ever had a pencil, but knows he was motivated in his writing by her expectations.

Luke and his friends took advantage of teachers who didn't demand respect.

They had a science teacher who the whole class would try to make think he had lost his hearing. They would mouth words silently and then act dumfounded when the teacher could not hear them.

A couple of pretty bright guys sat in the back row and sniffed chloroform until they fell off their chairs. Guys would take turns holding the teacher's door shut at noon so he couldn't go to lunch. They did these childish things because they could. The teacher never disciplined them, never turned them in to the principal and he gave them grades they didn't really earn. Luke didn't learn much in this class but a lot of it was his own fault. The teacher's weakness was no excuse for Luke's poor conduct.

Another time, in study hall Luke got into an argument with a female teacher over something and he was disrespectful. She turned him in to the principal, who Luke was to see with his parents the next day. That night at home he passionately made his case with his parents that he was being unfairly persecuted by this teacher. Luke felt that he had won his parents over to his side.

When they went to see the principal, the same one, by the way, who called Luke to his office on his first day of school as a first grader, it took less than two minutes into the meeting before Luke's parents had switched sides. The exact details of the punishment are somewhat forgotten, but it involved an apology and some restrictions for Luke at school and at home. There could have been a case here for double punishment, but Luke never pushed it!

Some of the things that Luke did that at the time seemed funny, but he now regrets doing them. Probably many kids did some things they aren't proud of and then they mature and learn to treat people the right way.

Typing class was fun and the inspiration here was that the teacher was young and good looking. At the end of the timed typing tests, as the teacher was collecting the papers in the front of the room, there were scattered, peck, peck, peck …. peck pecks as students tried to sneak in a couple of extra words. It would have been a bonus to have been kept after class by this teacher.

Even though Luke wasn't much into doing homework for school, he really liked to read.

He liked history and biographies, and he read any book in the library that was about sports. The Chip Hilton series was his favorite, Chip being a clean cut All-American boy who excelled in every sport.

At the newsstand Luke never missed an issue of Sport Magazine, The Sporting News and the yearly Street and Smith Baseball magazine. He read his share of comic books. There were "Superman" with Clark Kent and Lois Lane; "Archie" with Betty chasing Archie and Archie chasing Veronica and Jughead chasing anybody or nobody; "Donald Duck" with Daisy and the kids Huey, Dewey and Louie; and "Batman" with him and Robin running around in tights and capes.

There was a reading selection that wasn't available in the school library. Somehow, Luke and his friends got their hands on some "8 Page Bibles," which were sort of underground soft porno comic books. They were pocket size eight page books with titillating oversized sexual drawings. Luke took the lid off a shoe box and set the shoe box in the lid with three or four of these hidden between the lid and the box. He stashed this carefully in the bottom drawer of his bedroom dresser. He didn't factor in how thoroughly his mom sometimes cleaned and, of course, she discovered them. There was no way to escape. Luke's best effort was to say that he was keeping them for one of his friends. He knew it was pretty weak and it didn't do much to blunt the flack he caught. He survived.

In high school, the first paperback that Luke remembers kids passing around was "I the Jury" by Micky Spillane. There were some pages with the corner of the page turned down where the steamy scenes were located. By today's standards it was really very tame.

A list of quality books that Luke read before college would include "<u>Call of the Wild</u>," "<u>Black Beauty</u>," "<u>Tom Sawyer</u>" and "<u>To Kill a Mockingbird,</u> all were or have become, classics.

Luke had hall monitor duty for an hour right before lunch. His job was to sit at a desk looking down the main hallway to check to see if students had proper passes to be in the hall. To be outside of a classroom, a student needed a pass signed by a faculty member.

The school had an agriculture teacher who signed his first name with the initials TR sort of cleverly interlocked. Luke became really good at forging that TR signature and he had access to a pad of blank hall passes.

He told his friends about this and he became the hall-pass supplier for anyone who wanted to skip class. It got to the point where there were lots of kids running around the building and most of them had passes signed by TR. The ag teacher was asked why he was giving so many passes. He asked to see some of the passes and agreed that it was indeed his signature (a fleeting triumph for quality work), but he denied that he had issued many of the passes. The trail, of course, led back to Luke and among other things he lost his job as hall monitor.

The mistake Luke made was being too generous to too many friends. The passes should have been saved for special friends on really special occasions.

Luke played trumpet in the school band. When he started playing in grade school, his parents wanted him to play the drums. A drum was a lot less expensive and they had some doubts about his real interest in music.

He should have chosen to play the drums. He had never seen a dance band drummer with two or three drums and cymbals. All he focused on was the guy walking in the band with a drum hung around his neck.

Luke really never was very good on the trumpet. The only solo that he ever played was "<u>Abide With Me.</u>" It was embarrassing when the band director would hear something wrong and start the process of finding out who were the "clunkers." He would begin by having the first trumpets play. They were always very good. He would have the second trumpets play. No problems. Finally he would turn to Luke and the other two third trumpets. His search was successful, "these guys couldn't play."

Luke sometimes suggested to his fellow third-chair trumpeters that they just "mouth" as if they were playing so that there was no clunker noise to have to search for.

When Luke was a freshman in high school he was thrilled to find that he was on the list to dress for the first varsity football game. He was distressed the next day when he found that the band director needed bodies for the marching band and the coach had agreed to change his list. Now he was not dressing for the game. Luke went home and told his dad. They sold the trumpet the next day. Luke got into the football game as the holder on extra points.

At most schools student government was a big deal and Luke's school was no exception. In Luke's senior year there was a student council presidential election in the spring that created some excitement and controversy. It seemed to be a cut and dried election with a junior member of the student council running unopposed to move into the president's chair as a senior. He was definitely qualified and had the blessing of the high school principal. Sort of like having the support of a political party.

For something to do Luke, and a few other seniors decided to launch a write-in candidacy for a sophomore boy named Billy. He was a fun guy who was into sports and who everybody liked. He hadn't had a growth spurt yet so he was a little undersized, had no interest in student government nor any experiences that made him qualified. And most importantly, for whatever reason, he agreed to run.

A school assembly was to be held in the gymnasium for the candidates to be formally nominated and to make a brief acceptance speech. The night before the assembly Luke and his friends persuaded the janitor to let them in the gym. They had a big white bed sheet sign that said "WE BACK BILLY" rolled up and filled with little scraps of paper urging voters to write in Billy for president. They climbed into the rafters and positioned this rolled up sheet over the crowd. There was a "trip" cord attached and fed down the girder to the wall and it dropped to an out of the way spot on a side balcony.

After the candidates for treasurer, secretary and vice president had been nominated and made their speeches, the establishment candidate for president was nominated and made his acceptance speech. As a formality the principal asked if there were any further nominations. A pre-selected representative

of Luke's coalition came forward and nominated Billy. She simply stated that she was nominating Billy as a write-in candidate, "a candidate of the people."

With that, a "plant" on the balcony pulled the cord and the sign unfolded beautifully with confetti like campaign "literature" raining down on the crowd.

Billy then made one of the shortest and non-informational acceptance speeches in electoral history.

The election was a week away so the campaigning immediately began in earnest. The coalition had to not only sell their candidate, but educate voters to write Billy's name in and also mark the box with an X.

The seniors were allowed to vote to take advantage of their "maturity" and experience. The eighth graders, in the adjacent building, were allowed to vote because they would be a part of the high school the next year.

Billy's backers focused a lot of attention on the eighth graders as they were an extra large incoming class. The coalition had some status as it included star athletes and they gave away free candy bars with the implied obligation to accept the candy and vote for Billy. Some might call this a Chicago style strategy.

They had Billy promising to push some legitimate issues, but the underlying theme for him was that he was not the establishment's (principal's) candidate. There was no polling data, but Billy's handlers actually felt confident and some were even predicting a landslide victory.

Billy lost by three votes. There was some suspicion that there may have been some uncounted incorrectly marked ballots—in today's nomenclature, maybe some "hanging chads." Nobody asked for a recount, because the Supreme Court (the principal) would never have allowed one.

In the end it was probably a good result for the school.

Luke's class had a money-raising car wash in his small town. The rich guy in town had them wash his white Cadillac. After they had finished washing the car, Luke was to drive it back uptown to his office. He came to the first stop sign and stopped. One of Luke's classmates, a girl, was following to pick him up and bring him back to the car wash. She didn't stop and rear ended Luke, wrecking the rear end of the Cadillac. She jumped out and yelled, "What are you doing?" Luke said, "I stopped at the stop sign." She said "Luke, that is the first time in your life that you have ever stopped at a stop sign in this town!" She was right but legally, Luke was right. Everything turned out all right because the owner said that that was what he had insurance for and insisted on paying for the car wash.

There was no dress code anyone was aware of at the high school. Luke and his friends went through numerous fads. The basketball shoe was always white canvas Converse Chuck Taylor All-Stars. There was a period where all of the guys wore big black engineering boots, stomping down the hall like cowboys. Later they went through the blue suede and white buck shoe eras and finally black and white saddles. This was all in a period of about five years.

Everybody wore Levi's with no belt. It had to be Levi's, it couldn't just be blue jeans of any kind. Everyone wore them hung so low on their butt that it seemed that they were always on the verge of sliding down and off. This gave the illusion of really short legs and a long upper body. A lot of the way kids dressed was inspired by the Elvis Presley look. I guess the white bucks would be credited to Pat Boone.

The girls wore fairly tight sweaters, fairly tight straight skirts, and white bobby sox.

In P.E. class they wore an incredibly unattractive one piece gym outfit. Most of the girls Luke knew really disliked P.E.class and they hated the fact that they were penalized one letter grade every time they didn't take a shower.

How many people remember their first kiss, probably a lot more women than men. This is not about the chaste little party kisses, but their first "real" kiss. Luke certainly remembers his and it happened before high school.

There was a monster snow storm and none of the roads were open. Luke was in the sixth grade and a high school senior girl rode her horse into town. She was Luke's grade school girlfriend's older sister. She asked Luke to climb up behind her and go for a ride on the horse. They were riding through deep snow drifts and fell off and rolled through the snow. They were hollering and laughing when all of a sudden she gave Luke a long, wet kiss that included a little tongue. And then she did it again! Luke figured she did it again because the first one was so good!

She gave Luke a big grin and told him to try that on her little sister. He couldn't wait for his chance.

Chapter Four

It seems as if even in grade school, boys had a girl friend. As early as the first grade Luke would say that he "liked" Kay. It was uncertain whether she would have said she liked him. Then in the fourth or fifth grade it was Virginia and once in a while Luke would sit with her at the movie theatre.

When Luke was in the sixth grade he went for an older "woman", a seventh grader named Karen—his first kiss's little sister. Luke and Karen decided that she would wear his ring, which was a birthstone that his parents had given him. It was sort of like the high school kids did with their class ring when they were "going steady." The girl wrapped lots of tape around the under side of the ring to make it fit and then paint it red with nail polish.

Luke's mom asked him where his ring was and when she found that he had given it to Karen she was not happy. They were too young to go steady! His mom suggested that Luke buy her a friendship ring of some sort and get his back.

Luke wasn't sure how Karen would react to him asking for his ring back, but he did buy a friendship ring. They went on a school field trip and he put the ring in his pocket and was waiting for the right moment to give it to her and tactfully get his birthstone ring back. He didn't want it to seem as if he were a wimp whose mother told him what to do.

When the moment came and Luke reached in his pocket, the ring had been bent almost flat. The quality of the metal in the ring was obviously somewhat suspect. So there he was getting his ring back and trying to bend the one that is replacing it back into shape. It had a permanent crease on both sides and looked terrible. It was embarrassing to try to fit a semi-flat ring on Karen's little round finger. It was worthless and Luke tried to give her back his birthstone ring and of course he got the "your mom would not like it" routine.

It was a setback. From that point on it was uncertain whether Luke and Karen were "officially" going steady, but she was still his girlfriend.

It got even more complicated in high school when guys tried to juggle the hometown girl- friend with the prospects from neighboring towns.

The big weekend date was to drive about 30 miles to the city to see a movie. Luke got excited on warm summer nights when he and his date walked out of the theatre after seeing a movie. Special movies like "Blackboard Jungle." ONE TWO THREE O"CLOCK FOUR O"CLOCK ROCK! Sidney Poitier, Glenn Ford and Vic Morrow were the stars and music by Bill Haley and the Comets. This movie ushered in a whole new era of Rock n' Roll for his generation.

After the movie Luke and his date would make about 17 cruises through the Steak n Shake drive in to see who was there—and to be seen themselves.

Finally, he would back his car into a parking space and leave the lights on for curb service. A car-hop waitress would take their order and serve them. The order was almost always a steakburger, fries and a shake and more importantly it was a chance to see the kids from the other towns drive through.

In the summertime the evening would end at the Putt Putt golf and driving range, and then Luke might take his date to a secluded parking spot for a few kisses before taking her home. In the winter when there was no Putt Putt golf, school was on so he had to be home earlier—or he had a little more time at the secluded parking spot.

A pre-baseball game stop for Luke would be the A & W Root Beer stand to get a coney dog and a mug of root beer and to tease the car-hops. The car radio was always on with tunes like "Shaboom" by the Crew Cuts or "The Great Pretender" by the Platters.

What could be better?

Chapter 5

Sports in school were a big part of growing up in a small town, even though there were no sports teams for the girls and really only four for the boys: football, basketball, baseball and track.

They did have a physical education class co-ed track meet. One of the girls running the final leg of a relay fell head first on the cinder track as she strained to reach the finish line. She imbedded cinders in ugly cuts on her elbows and knees. Female athletes being injured in sports now is common, but back then it was a real trauma. There were a lot of tears and a lot of the guys willing to check out the leg wounds.

When the high school consolidated they started a football program. One of the schools had previously played six-man football, but it was a new experience for nearly all of the farm kids.

Many of the helmets were suspension type helmets which meant that there was an outer shell and then an inner strap that fit around a player's head. It was sort of like a "bobble head" feeling and a good solid hit would really "ring your bell."

There were no face masks which meant a number of teeth losses and broken noses. The hip pads were sort of like strapping on a six-gun belt as opposed to today's elastic girdle concept. When a player was tackled, the hip pad belt would often slip off or be spun around so the buckle was on his hip or even all of the way around to the middle of his back.

In this era, good sportsmanship was important. When a player scored a touchdown there was a sense of personal humility. There was no spiking the ball, chest bumping or sideline dance that drew attention to one's self and ridiculed the opponent. ESPN, bad examples and a lack of good manners were far in the future.

The school's first football field tilted down hill (or up hill in the other direction) at what seemed like a twenty five degree slant. That meant that when a team was going uphill into a prevailing wind it was really hard to move the ball.

There were other schools' fields that Luke's team played on that were worse.

One of the schools had an 80 yard field. This meant that when a ball-carrier crossed the goal line he had not scored. His team had a first down on the 20 yard line. Football fans have heard of prevent defenses, this was a prevent field.

One school had a dry creek bed (on non-rainy days) that ran across the field at about the spot where extra points were attempted. The kicker had to be able to get extra lift to get the ball high enough to get out of the creek and over the cross bar.

Finally, one school's field was marked off in an "active" cow pasture. No attempt was made to remove the cow patties. This made it treacherous to plant and cut, and made the ball carrier think twice before diving for a first down.

Luke could get a yearbook out and relate something about a game winning shot in basketball or a touchdown in football, but it was the bus rides and the off the field team experiences that were memorable.

After about the first four basketball games of Luke's freshman year, the varsity coach decided to have him dress for his first varsity game After having played in the preliminary freshman-sophomore game Luke suited up for the varsity game. He was thrilled, of course, and took his seat at the end of the bench knowing that there was no way that he was going to get to play.

Luke was also hungry, so he asked one of the cheerleaders to buy him a Clark bar. He quietly unwrapped the candy and took a big bite. At that exact moment, the coach called his name to come sit by him. He was putting Luke into the game! Luke threw the rest of the candy bar under the bleachers and ran down to sit by the coach. If you have ever eaten a Clark bar, you know how chewy it is to eat.

Luke turned his head away trying to gum it up to the point where he could swallow it and his coach says, "Are you feeling alright?" Luke nodded his head vigorously and mumbled "umhuh."

"Okay," his coach said, Get in there for Pinky." So Luke made his high school varsity debut with a Clark bar stuck to the roof of his mouth!

Luke had another stressful basketball issue that had nothing to do with the ball or the hoop or playing defense. The subject area is a little delicate, but dealing with it was traumatic for a young high school kid.

He had this sharp pain in his "behind" so he finally told his dad that he thought he had a boil in his butt. His dad's immediate reaction was that Luke had a case of the "piles." (Another word for hemorrhoids.)   He sent Luke to the town's doctor who confirmed that he had a severe case of hemorrhoids that would need to be cut out.

It was so painful to walk, let alone run, that Luke would have agreed to about any solution. The doctor decided to perform an outpatient procedure in his office. As Luke was lying on the table waiting, the doctor walked in with a huge long needle. Pretty much knowing where the doctor was going to stick that needle, Luke said "Doc, forget the needle, just cut'em out."

The doctor said, "Son, there are not enough men in that pool hall across the street to hold you down if I don't give you this shot." The injection was extremely painful, but over fairly quickly. There was a lot of bleeding and Luke's team had a game the next night at home and they would be wearing white uniforms. The doctor told Luke that it would not be healed completely and would be sore, but that he could play.

Luke asked the doctor how he could bandage the area to keep from bleeding through his white uniform pants. The doctor went into his storeroom and brought Luke a box of sanitary napkins. Luke said, "Wait a minute, I'm not going to wear Kotex." The doctor told him that he really had no other choice.

Most times the varsity team goes to the locker room to get dressed at the end of the third quarter of the junior varsity game. Luke sneaked down to the locker room right after the half to get "fitted" and dressed before any of his teammates were around.

He played well, the protection soaked up all of the blood and none of his teammates ever knew about it. He came away with a tiny bit of an understanding of what a female has to deal with in life.

Basketball rules have changed so many times that the way the game is played now is different in many ways from that of Luke's days. There was a time when the coach was not allowed to talk to the players during a time-out. The players would gather in a huddle under the hoop and talk things over amongst themselves. A rival high school rolled a small wicker basket with towels out to the players and Luke's team's fans swore that the coach was sending strategy notes in the basket.

If you think about it, this might be a good rule today, as coaches call time-out on nearly every possession in the final minutes of the game to micro-manage every play and the game goes on forever.

After being indoors all winter, almost all of the school's athletes participated in a spring sport. One year there were only 13 players on the high school baseball team. The 13th player was a small freshman who loved baseball. He was a huge Cubs fan, so he had no real concept of winning baseball. It was thought that he got a high school uniform mostly because he knew how to keep a scorebook.

One nice day in May at corn-planting time, he went to the coach and said that he couldn't play because he had to help his dad plant corn. The coach told him that he already had so many guys committed to planting that if this kid didn't go we would not have nine players and would have to forfeit the game.

When the kid told his dad that he was actually going to play, he was freed from his corn chores so he could play. He played right field (Babe Ruth's position). He walked once and got picked off first, but his team won the game and they named him MVP because if he hadn't played they would have had to forfeit the game.

Golf was nothing in Luke's life until after he graduated from high school. He was never at a country club for any reason, let alone to play or watch golf. The only person he knew who played golf was an attorney on the Sunday men's baseball team. The only reason Luke knew he played golf was that he was late for batting practice because he played golf on Sunday mornings.

Luke read about Sam Snead and Ben Hogan, and there was a movie, "Follow the Sun," about the comeback Ben Hogan made after a terrible auto accident (starring Glen Ford and Donna Reed) but he had no concept of the skills or strategies of the game.

The school's physical education teacher tried a six-week section on golf. He had his class hitting plastic practice balls with a driver. The students were so bored that when he left the kids alone they divided into teams and played field hockey with the golf equipment.

The teacher finally took the class to a golf course in Fairbury, a close-by town, to play nine holes. The course had sand greens. The golfers would mark their ball on the green/sand and then use a smoothing tool to smooth about a two-foot wide path from their ball to the hole. The tool was a flat board with a handle. Luke wasn't impressed at all with the game. Arnold Palmer playing in the Masters tournament finally got his attention.

A friend of Lukes, whose father owned a hardware store, had tennis racquets and a net. He and Luke tied one end of the net to an abandoned loading dock and the other to an apricot tree.

The playing surface was gravel and they scratched out court lines with a sharp stick. (This was a farm town version of the clay courts at the French Open.) Tennis was something different to do, but Luke and his friends had no role models in the sport.

At that time, golf and tennis were definitely not farm town sports.

Baseball and in lots of cases softball, was surely the national pastime in the small towns.

There was a full schedule of weekend tournaments at the adult level with the local church's women members raising funds with a concession stand.

There were entry fees and cash prizes to the winning team. Most of the small town teams would fill the line-up card with local players and then hire a pitcher. These pitchers were so overpowering that most of the games were dominated by the bunt and run.

In Luke's town there were two teams, one from the Lutheran church and one sponsored by the gear company in town. These were men's leagues, but from about the fifth grade on Luke was there early to shag balls in batting practice and play catch with the players. He would count the players as they arrived, always hoping that they would come up short and he would get to play. It happened at least a half dozen times a summer and Luke would get to play. Sometimes it was only for a few innings if a player got there late.

The Corn Belt League was an adult men's Sunday afternoon baseball league.

They played a doubleheader every Sunday with another area small town team. The uniforms they wore were made of stifling hot heavy wool with a different sponsor's name on the back of each uniform. The sponsoring merchant would pay for the uniform. Luke was the regular shortstop when he was a freshman in high school. His uniform was provided by McLean County Service Company, his dad's employer. All of the businesses in town sponsored a uniform. The neatest was the tavern's which simply said, BLATZ BEER.

One Sunday in Luke's first year in the league his team let a pop-up fall uncaught in the infield. Even though Luke was the youngest player in the infield by 10 years, when he got home after the game his dad told him that as the shortstop he should take charge and make sure that all infield pop-ups are caught. The next Sunday Luke spiked the first basemen in foul territory outside first base making the catch.

The league was a really-low budget operation. In the seventh inning of the game the manager would take off his hat and pass it among the crowd for donations. They used this cash for bats, balls and equipment. A baseball bat then cost about six dollars and every Sunday a few would be broken. The team had a dozen bats and most players had one or two of their own. They really didn't want to share their personal bat for fear it would be broken. A dozen metal bats today would cost over $2000. You would now have to use a wheelbarrow to collect enough money to operate.

The league rule was that the home team had to supply three new game balls for each game. Once in a while the game would be delayed while all of the players from both teams were in the bean field adjacent to the ball diamond looking for a game ball.

If all three balls were lost, both teams checked their ball bags to find a decent ball to finish the game.

In a neighboring town in this league, foul balls on the third base side would end up in a small grove of trees. Some high school kids found a dead white cat. They buried it with just its head sticking out of the ground in the grove. The next Sunday a ball chaser came screaming out of the trees after reaching down to pick up what he mistook for a baseball.

The bases were secured with metal stakes driven into the ground and would often come loose. There were a few arguments as to whether a base runner slid off the bag or whether the bag slid away from the base runner.

When Luke first started playing baseball, players would leave their gloves on the field when their team came to bat. The shortstop would just toss his glove somewhere behind second base and the outfielders would just toss them behind where they stood. If a batted ball hit a glove or a player stumbled over one it was simply a part of the game. There was no penalty.

When the rule was changed to make players bring their gloves with them to the bench each inning, a lot of players complained. They felt it was too much extra work to lug that glove in and out every inning.

There were some real characters in the league. One was a pitcher who pitched with a cigarette hanging out of his mouth the entire game. One of the managers in the league wore argyle sox instead of baseball hose and his steal signal was winding his watch.

There was a state representative who played third base for one of the teams.

They had a regular umpire in the league who everybody called Hornsby. This politician- third baseman took the first pitch which looked real low and Hornsby hollered "strike one." The batter stepped out and glared at Hornsby, then got back into the box and waited for the next pitch which was a little lower. Hornsby said "strike two."

The batter went wild and he said, "Wait a minute." He stepped back into the batter's box and without the pitcher throwing he took a giant swing and said, "Strike three, I'm out."

Hornsby said, "You're God damned right you're out, you're out of the ballgame!"

Fun at the old ball park!

A few of the better players from this league played in the Municipal League in Bloomington. This was the "big leagues" to the area's amateur baseball players. It was a city league in which most of the players were graduates of the city's high schools or players from the two local colleges. It was really competitive with a number of former minor league players involved. Each team would play night ball on the university field a couple of times a week.

Luke was thrilled to be asked to play shortstop for a team called the Moose Lodge when he was a junior in high school. He had memories of his dad taking him to one of these games when he was in grade school. Luke remembered how impressed he was when his high school coach, who pitched in the league, was paid $15 in the parking lot after the game for pitching. This was big-time stuff to Luke.

The real big-time sports stuff, though, was the fun Luke had with his teammates. Almost all of the athletes played all sports so they were with each other all year.

It wasn't the win or losses, it was the friendships and relationships at practices, in the locker rooms, in the dugouts, and on bus rides. It was joking with each other, laughing together and sometimes crying together.

Chapter 6

Being a farm community, the 4-H clubs were really popular for many reasons. It was an opportunity for the farm kids to learn to handle livestock and to show off their cattle, hogs or sheep at the county, and then the state, fairs. A lot of farmers were in the livestock business and showing the Grand Champion heifer or boar was a big deal.

The lure for Luke was to play on the 4-H softball team and to be able camp out at the fair for three or four nights with his project and so he needed a livestock project. Since he lived in town, he was in a bind to come up with something. Luke knew that nobody stayed overnight at the fair with their garden display or with their electrical wiring experiment.

In Luke's first year, his dad agreed to buy him a couple of Hampshire barrows. They were black and white with a white stripe around their bellies. Barrows are to the pig community what steers are to the cattle community. For anyone without a farming background, these pigs were "fixed" so that they had no breeding capabilities.

Later, when Luke was a few years older, he helped some farmers with this procedure. It is done when the pigs are very young and it wasn't a particularly fun day for the pig. Luke did not do any of the actual cutting, rather, his role was more of an aider and abetter and could be best described as a "pig holder." It was sort of like driving the getaway car.

Luke had a farm friend who told him about helping perform this procedure on sheep. The friend said that the target organs are in such a slippery gel that the farmer exposes them by cupping them in his hand and then extracts them with his teeth. Whoa… Luke didn't think he could sign on for the lead role in this type of operation. In some western states, these organs are fried and served as Rocky Mountain Oysters. (It must be an acquired taste).

To house his pigs, Luke and his dad fenced in the area underneath the petroleum tanks at their FS petroleum storage plant. These were the large storage tanks where fuel oil and gasoline were stored until loaded to deliver to the farmers. Luke was responsible for feeding and watering the two hogs. Luke never got around to naming them, but by the end of the summer his dad had and the first name of both of them was "Stinkin."

With a big hog barn right across the road east of town, the pig smell was not new to Luke's town. This pig smell was right under their noses though, and with them every day that summer. It was almost as if Luke and his dad would rather lean over the tanks on the truck and fill their nostrils with gas or diesel fuel fumes to escape the stench.

As the time for the county fair rolled around Luke and his dad tried to decide which of the hogs he should enter. One was kind of scrawny while the other one was really not a bad looking animal—so Luke was told—but it had a little bit of a gimpy hind leg. It was not really that noticeable if the pig stood still or walked slowly so they decided to go with this pig and take a chance on the gimpy leg.

Staying at the fair was really fun. Just hanging out in the livestock tents with kids from all over the county was great. Luke and his friends climbed over the fence and sneaked into the outdoor theatre located next to the fairgrounds, and cruised the carnival midway following girls around. Luke had fun watching his serious 4-H friends show their livestock and he watched the grandstand shows and the horse show.

Of course, there was that brief moment when he had to prepare his animal for the show ring. To get his animal ready, the first thing he had to do was get a bucket of suds and a garden hose and give it a bath. After this ordeal, the white splash around the belly was dusted with white talcum powder to highlight the contrast between the black and white. It was sort of like putting on make-up before a big date.

The tools used to show a pig were a cane and a "show-board." That may not be the proper name for this piece of equipment, but it was a wide board with a handle at the top to place in front of your pig to force it to change direction.

Luke had practiced his show skills a little under the fuel tanks and actually scouted a few of the other breed's show-men. It seemed as if the competitors tried to maneuver their pig in front of the judge as much as possible to make a good impression. The judge would walk around with a frown on his face, deep in thought and every so often point at a hog, which in effect eliminated it from the competition. When he got to the final five which won ribbons and prize money, he first directed number five into a pen, then number four and so on, until it was down to two pigs and he then grandly pointed at the winner.

Luke decided on a little bit of a different strategy. He did everything he could to maneuver his pig so that the judge didn't see him. He felt that the less the judge saw his pig the less chance he would be eliminated. He also knew that the more exposure his pig got the greater the odds were that the gimpy leg would be discovered. His strategy needed to work because Luke's entry was not in the same class with the serious farm kids' pigs.

As the competition began there was a crowded corral of about 20 pigs, somehow Luke and his pig made it down to the final six, mostly because Luke had kept him pretty well wedged in a corner. When the judge finally had his first real chance to eyeball Luke's pig, it was almost laughable to see his look of "where the hell did you come from?" The judge dismissed Luke's pig with a wave of his cane just one spot away from a "ribbon" pen.

There was a "showman" prize in the hog competition and Luke's friends thought that he should have won. He took an undersize competitor with a gimpy leg and just missed finishing in the money!

That was the first and last year for the Fuel Tank Hog Farm. Luke and his dad sold the entire herd (two pigs) and started a search for a new project for the next year's fair. Luke had to have a project because he was the starting shortstop on the 4-H softball team.

They settled on rabbits. It was a compromise deal. There was no record of any kids actually staying overnight at the fair with their rabbits. Luke agreed to become a rabbit rancher with the proviso that his parents would let him take his sleeping cot to the fair. They agreed. He didn't actually sleep in the rabbit tent, as he would have really been conspicuous. Instead he went back to the pig tent to bunk with some of his farm friends.

Luke bought a New Zealand White buck and three does. He fenced in an area near the alley by the family garage, built four rabbit hutches and he was in the rabbit business. Rabbits are really clean animals and rabbit manure is little pellets that are relatively odor free, unless you let them build up in the hutch.

Luke had some chores in connection with his 4-H rabbit project. The hutches needed to be regularly cleaned and the rabbit manure spread on the family's garden.

When the next August rolled around Luke had three fairly good sized litters of baby rabbits. He chose one of his older does and a young junior doe to enter as his county fair project.

The judging of rabbits was quite different from that of pigs. Competitors simply walked up to the table and set their rabbits in assigned boxes and the judge took over. You didn't have to herd the little critter around the ring like you did the pig. Really, they all look alike and it amazed Luke that when all was said and done everybody left with his or her own rabbit.

The judge took a quick check of the rabbit's sex, felt for gimpy legs—Luke was okay in that regard that year—ruffled the fur a number of times and felt for a solid set of shoulders. As with pigs, it was an elimination process.

Luke's older doe evidently had a bad hair day and was eliminated early in the judging.

His junior doe, though, turned out to be a superstar, and not only won first prize but won Grand Champion junior doe. She won a blue ribbon, a small trophy and $15 prize money. In the mid-1950s this was really good money. Luke, of course, was modest as he accepted the accolades of his colleagues in the rabbit raising industry. At that time no one knew what a really amazing job he had done.

As soon as Luke returned home from the fair he sold off all of the young rabbits and kept only the original four and, of course, the superstar of the stable, the Grand Champion junior doe. It was important not to become too emotionally attached to the "herd", because, sadly, they were sold to the restaurant industry for white meat.

The next spring when Luke's champion young doe came of age he introduced her to his buck in hopes that she wanted to start a family. Nothing happened, so Luke took her to his rabbit supplier in the next town to see if maybe another partner would be the answer. The supplier/mentor called to tell him that the reason the doe wasn't conceiving was that it was in fact a he. This buck had won best of breed doe. Luke thought it might have been the broad shoulders!

The judges sex check was pretty fleeting and they surely missed something. How embarrassed Luke would have been had the judge rejected her/him in front of all of the contestants.

As an exhibitor Luke was certainly getting the best out of his talent. In his two years he guided a gimpy legged, under talented pig to within one slot of placing and won best of breeds doe with a buck. Imagine what he could have done if he ever had championship material!

Luke was always looking for opportunities in sports, so 4-H softball was another bunch of games to look forward to every summer. His team was playing a 4-H league game a few days before the fair one year, and Luke asked the best player on the other team what his project was for the fair. The kid said that his project was vegetables. Luke knew that the kid lived close to the business district in his small town, so he asked him where his garden was located. The kid responded that he didn't have a garden. He said that he got his vegetables for the fair from his father's store the day before the fair.

Luke was sure the kid had a competitive display. His secret was safe with Luke.

A sidebar to Luke's rabbit raising operation was about how he raised a duck. At a small town summer carnival Luke won a little duckling by throwing a coin on a plate. It was probably the only bird that he really didn't fear, at least while it was a little fuzzy duckling. He brought it home and let it run loose in the fenced enclosure where he had his rabbit hutches. In a couple of years Luke had a full grown duck on his hands waddling around making a racket and at that point he was viewing it more as a bird than as a lovable fuzzy. The duck droppings were not particularly pleasant.

Chapter Six

Luke came home from school one night and the duck was missing. His mom and dad told him that the duck must have gotten through the fence and been killed by a dog. The next weekend the family had a big turkey dinner and it wasn't Thanksgiving. At some point Luke became aware that their "turkey" dinner was his former furry pet. Luke was just glad that he didn't know at dinner time.

The county fair always had a wholesome family feel to it. Later in the summer at a few of the small town carnivals there were some "girlie" shows that weren't so high class.

It was pretty much known that the night to go to one of these shows was the carnival's last night in town. The city fathers or church groups couldn't kick you out of town if you were leaving anyway. It was for adults only, but if you had the cash for a ticket you were an adult.

The first portion of the show was a teaser, mostly dancing and shaking. Then the emcee announced that for a few extra bucks you could stay for the final act.

The rest was really crude; farm animals were included in the act. Some of the females were pretty bad. If the authorities had raided the show the No. 1 charge might have been cruelty to animals.

Newspaper delivery crew and "helper."

Chapter 7

Luke's first money-making job was a newspaper route. He had the exclusive contract to deliver both the Bloomington Daily Pantagraph and the Chicago Daily News for the town. The Pantagraph sold for 30 cents a week and the Daily News for 45 cents a week. Luke's high water marks were 52 subscriptions for the Pantagraph and 12 for the Daily News. The Pantagraph subscribers included the tavern, the bank and both grain elevators. Of the 12 Daily News subscribers, 11 also took the Pantagraph. Luke had one truck driver subscribing only to the Daily News.

The Pantagraph had its own truck that dropped the newspapers off at the post office. The first potential crisis came every morning when Luke counted the Pantagraphs to make certain that they had indeed sent him 52. If he was short one paper, his family quickly read theirs and then delivered it to their next-door neighbor. If he was short more than one he would try to think if he knew of anyone who was out of town and wouldn't miss that day's delivery, or he would call one of his family's better friends and try to work out a sharing plan for that day. It didn't happen often, but it caused a flurry of administrative strategy when it did.

Another reason for carefully counting the papers was that at the end of the route if Luke had any left, he knew that he had missed someone. Normally, by noon his mom had received a complaining phone call which cleared up the situation.

It was really pretty easy. If he hit the tavern and the bank uptown first, and then walked down one side of Main Sreet and back up the other side he had delivered 60 per cent of the route. After that, riding his bike (and in later years in his car) he could cover the two side streets, swing by the elevators and then finish with the seven houses on his small block. There was a time when his older sister shared his route and handled Main Street, and later when he was in high school on many mornings his mom would let him sleep in a little and handle the trip up and down Main Street.

Luke's Saturday morning job was collecting for the paper.

Many of the older ladies on his route paid the minimum 30 cents each week. They would search for their purse and then dig down into a tiny coin purse for the 30 cents. Luke would tear off and give them the tiny weekly tab. Paying by the week in many cases was a chance for these people to visit with someone for a few minutes. A strip of tabs was $1.50 and would mean that Luke didn't have to collect again for five weeks. If he had an opportunity he would push this option. With the older folks, it was a problem if for some reason Luke had missed collecting for three or four weeks because they then couldn't understand why it was more than 30 cents.   Even when he was able to show them that the tabs for the weeks in doubt were still in the book, he left many times under a cloud of suspicion.

The Daily News arrived each morning by U.S mail. No mail on Sundays meant no Daily News to deliver.

Luke's truck driver customer who only subscribed to the Chicago paper had him leave his paper each morning at the tavern. He always paid Luke in advance. Luke would make certain to arrange to collect from the trucker later Saturday afternoon at the tavern after he had tipped a few. He would, with a little slur to his speech, ask Luke "How mush do I owe you?" Luke would respond that, "You usually pay $4.50 for 10 weeks." Many times he would hand Luke a 10 dollar bill and say, "Aw hell, jush keep the change" This is probably the only tip Luke ever received, except for Christmas, when he made out really well.

Luke collected from his next-door-neighbor at his black-smith shop. He was a bachelor with a somewhat gruff disposition. His shop was truly an old-time blacksmith shop and many times when Luke stopped to collect, the blacksmith would have plowshares buried in a white-hot fire and be pounding one into shape with a heavy hammer. His big hang-up was when his Daily News was not delivered on a holiday. He would tell Luke and any farmers who happened to be in the shop at the time how the "fat cats" in Chicago were buying new cars with the money they were saving not printing those papers. He would withhold nine cents from his payment as his protest. It didn't hit Luke until after he had given up his route that the reason he didn't get a paper on holidays was because there was no U.S. mail on holidays and the papers simply did not make it to town. If you think about it, though, the papers never arrived in the mail a day late either. This seems to indicate that nobody ever put them in the mail. Maybe the fat cat theory had some validity.

The Pantagraph rewarded carriers with a certain amount of seniority with a trip to Chicago for a few days. This was Luke's first real trip to the big city. They went to Wrigley Field where they saw the Dodgers play the Cubs. Jackie Robinson played then for the Dodgers and Andy Pafko was the Cubs' star. The carriers ate their meals at the Forum cafeteria and stayed at the Sherman Hotel where they, of course, dropped water balloons from the 25th-floor windows. They went to the Riverview Amusement Park and rode the "Bobs" roller coaster (first and last roller coaster ride in Luke's lifetime). Finally, they walked over to State Street to the Chicago Theatre. The live show was Mickey Rooney and Jackie Gleason in a shoe salesman skit. Fran Warren sang the song from Moulin Rouge and the movie was the "Diplomatic Courier" starring Tyrone Power. Only later did Luke realize what a big deal this was for a kid his age.

They also attended a Chicago Symphony Orchestra concert. Luke's biggest memory of it was a bag lady who sat in the front row and picked her nose the entire performance.

It is widely held that having a paper route teaches a kid discipline and a little business sense. Maybe it wasn't so in Luke's case. His mom and dad bailed him out so many times with the delivery responsibility and often he would count on collecting far ahead to be able to turn in funds to the Pantagraph and still borrow available cash for a Saturday night date. It is called deficit spending. Luke wasn't saddened when he passed the job off to another kid in town.

Luke and his sister also mowed a good number of lawns. The ladies they mowed for were Mae, Delsy, Claudia, Eliza and Babe. One would mow while the other trimmed. Luke hated the trimming assignment. The top pay-day was $4.50 for Mae's yard. You could get 15 weeks of the Pantagraph for that!

The walnut crop created the first entrepreneurship opportunity for Luke and his friends. The plan was to gather the walnuts in bushel baskets, hull them and then sell them for $3.00 a bushel. It took no time to gather a basket of un-hulled walnuts, but it took forever to fill a bushel basket after peeling off the hulls. Even using gloves, the walnut stain on the kids' hands was severe and would only wear off with time. Luke really loved the smell of walnuts. Along with gasoline, burning leaves and pig manure (details later), it remains one of the odors of his youth. Even today if he picks up a walnut, he seemingly has to smell it and try to convince his grandkids to agree with him that it smells good.

The kids attempted to streamline their hulling operation by emptying the collections onto the street near the grain elevator so that the large grain hauling trucks would run over them. They could then simply pick up the freed walnuts. It was an assembly line concept.

Every year selling walnuts seemed like a good idea, yet Luke and his friends sold only a few bushels.

Living in a farm town there were always farm- related jobs available. Farmers were always looking for crews of kids to cut "volunteer" or "wild" corn and weeds out of the bean fields or to cut "butterprint" out of the cornfields. The farmers referred to this task as walking beans. It was a repetitive and seemingly endless job, walking back and forth down the rows hacking at unwanted plant life.

It is really a wonder that somebody didn't get a hand cut off in these field-clearing jobs. The kids were armed with razor-sharp machetes and, particularly in the cornfields, they were slashing weeds in fairly close quarters. Luke was hampered in his first "butterprint" cutting job because he didn't know what butterprint plants looked like. He missed the first day of work, which was what they would now call the orientation. He didn't want to admit that he didn't know a butterprint plant from any other weed so he just slashed away at about anything. At the noon break, Charlie, who was the boss, said that he had back checked and we were missing lots of butterprint plants. Luke figured he probably was the culprit.

Luke had a friend whose dad was a farmer and both he and his dad detested walking beans. They would prefer to be at the tavern playing gin rummy or at the pool hall shooting pool. They had a landlady, though, who hated to see a bean field that wasn't clean. One of her fields rose steadily to a crest of a hill from the road. They would clean the field only as far as she could see, to the crest of the hill. When the landlady drove by her field, she was surely impressed by how clean her tenant farmer kept the field. She wouldn't want any of her friends to think she had "dirty beans."

Working conditions for detasseling corn were the worst. In the early morning the corn was wet and in just a few minutes everyone's clothes were soaked. Then, as the sun came out they would bake. If the crew was walking there was absolutely no air and if anyone was under six feet tall it was a real stretch to reach up to pull the tassel. If they rode a machine, the sharp edges of the corn leaves left cuts on their hands and of course the sun beat down unmercifully. Some girls would tape their boyfriend's name on their leg, or paint it on with nail polish and use baby oil and iodine as tanning aids. When they removed the tape or paint, the boyfriend's name stood out on the tanned leg like a white tattoo. No one used "sun block," and no one ever thought about skin cancer. Kids were told that being out in the sun was good for them. Wide-brimmed straw hats were worn only for relief from the heat.

Baling hay was really a group effort around the town. There were about eight farmers who worked together to bale each other's hay and store it in the barns. It is unclear how they decided whose hay fields were baled first. They may have had some sort of pecking order that Luke was not aware of, or maybe it was just which fields were ready first. It was important that the hay was dry enough on a particular day before starting to bale. Wet hay in the barn could explode. Luke often thought he would like to have had a dollar for every time he heard one of the farmers say, "Remember, it is really only 10 o'clock by the sun" in reference to daylight savings time. I guess one extra hour of drying made a difference.

The eight farmers each had a full-time hired man and they all hired one of the town kids. This meant they had a work crew of at least 24 people. You would have to have worked a regular baling job to appreciate what this meant. If you were hired for a normal baling job, two guys would work all day to load the rack and most often load four bales high with a tie. A tie is farmer talk for one bale stacked in the middle to keep bales from falling off the side of the hayrack.

With all of the help they had the rack loaders would load two racks (three high with a tie) and then sit in the shade and rest while two racks were being loaded. With two balers going and a couple of the younger kids to drive tractors to haul the loaded racks to the barn, the field part of the operation used a dozen guys.

The other 12 men were assigned to the barn to unload the racks and stack the hay in the hayloft. Three guys set the hay hooks on the racks and the other nine guys worked in the haymow. Really, they had people falling all over each other. They would let about 10 loaded hayracks back up while they played poker, then race to unload those ten so that they could get back to the card game.

Most of the guys in the game were the "hired men." A lot of them it seemed were from the hills of Kentucky. Luke often heard one farmer say to another unkindly, "Oh hell, he's just a damn Kentuckian!" The damn Kentuckians taught Luke to play poker and he paid for his lessons.

Luke was making less than a dollar an hour for his work. They played only nickel, dime and quarter-on-the-last-card poker, but most times he lost more playing cards than he made baling hay. Luke never seemed to be able to take advantage of a good hand. He was never in a position with a good hand to raise the bet. In one game he finally was dealt a full house. He checked and after others bet, he raised. All hell broke loose, "Whoa, we don't check and raise around here," everybody screamed and they all reached into the pot and took out their money. The one great hand Luke had that day and he blew it. Luke is a decent poker player now, at least partially from lessons learned the hard way while baling hay.

There was a hay baling incident that had a "Keystone Cops" kind of tenor to it that could have been serious.

One of the farmers, whose first name was Sykes, was driving a tractor pulling a loaded hayrack heading to the barn to be unloaded. A thunder storm blew in pretty much without warning and Sykes stopped the tractor, jumped off and crawled under the hayrack to get out of the rain and seek protection from lightning.

Split second timing is important in how this story played out. Just a few seconds after Sykes dove off the left side of the tractor to get under the rack, another farmer named Roy, whose view was blocked by the loaded rack, jumped out of his pick-up truck and on to the tractor from the right side. He never saw Sykes at all.

Roy's intent was to ignore the storm and heroically get the wagon to the barn to keep the hay from getting soaked. He ran over Sykes!

Miraculously, Sykes escaped with only a few broken ribs, but from that point on whenever it started to rain, someone would say, "where the hell is Sykes?"

Chapter Seven

A highlight of the hay baling day was mid-afternoon when the farmers' wives would bring a big lunch to the field. One hired man's great claim to fame was that he could spread his mouth wide enough to eat five sandwiches at once. Everyone has a niche!

Luke was 14 years old in the summer after his freshman year when he was hired by a farmer who raised Spotted Poland China hogs along with his grain farming. The farmer's son, who was a high school senior, was going to Minnesota fishing for three weeks and Luke was hired as his replacement. The farmer loaned Luke a homemade, hand painted powder blue motor bike to ride back and forth from home to the farm. Luke started at 6 o'clock in the morning while it was still dark and quitting time was whenever the evening chores ended, often after dark. His pay was 5 dollars a day.

The first day the farmer asked Luke if he could drive a tractor even though he knew Luke wasn't old enough to have a driver's license. Luke had driven tractors for at least a year hauling in corn and beans so the answer was yes. The plan was for Luke to go to the field and cultivate corn. The farmer put Luke on an Allis Chalmers tractor with a two-row cultivator which in itself was a problem, because the clutch and break pedals were so far from the seat that Luke had to virtually sit on his back to reach them. He explained to Luke that all he had to do was sight the row of new corn through a guide on the right and cultivate up and back in the field. About mid-morning, he joined Luke in the field with another tractor and right away Luke saw him standing on the seat of his tractor waving his arms. Luke tentatively waved back, being careful to keep the corn row on the right centered in the guide. The farmer's waving became a little more frantic so Luke decided that he wasn't just saying hello. He stopped and waited until the farmer made his way to his tractor. The farmer asked Luke to look back at the area that he had cultivated and when he did he saw that every other row had been plowed out.

The farmer hadn't explained the concept of "planter rows." The cultivator had to start on the same two rows that the planter had planted so that the plows on the left would miss the same two rows as those on the right. Luke was so focused on following directions and "sighting" the row on his right that he never thought to look back at his work. Luke hadn't been clued into the technicalities well enough and this cost time and money for a few acres of replanting.

On the second day, Luke's next tractor job involved watering the hogs in the hog lot. He filled the water wagon up with water and drove to the hog lot where he would estimate that there were about 200 medium size hogs milling around waiting for the water. It was blazing hot and the hogs really needed a drink.

Backing a wagon with a tractor takes some skill and, indeed, a little practice. Luke had neither. To unload the water the wagon had to be backed up to the water tank. Luke knew that he needed to turn the tractor opposite the direction that he wanted to back the wagon to go but it wasn't working. He had to go at creep speed because of all the pigs milling around the tractor and wagon. Early on he was really being careful, but as he became frustrated he started going faster as he straightened the tractor up to try again.

As luck would have it, Luke ran over one of the hogs.

He unhooked the wagon and drove in to tell his boss that he had run over the pig. The farmer asked Luke how badly the pig was hurt and Luke told him he thought pretty bad. It was bleeding a lot from the mouth and not moving. The farmer said for Luke to hook up the hayrack and go out and pick up the pig. He went on to tell Luke to go out behind the corn crib, kill the pig and bury it.

"Kill the pig?" Luke asked, "How do I do that?" He said that Luke should get a big hammer from the tool shed and hit the pig on the forehead. Luke expressed some doubts about his ability and, indeed, his eagerness to attempt this, but the farmer pretty much let Luke know that he had created the problem and that he would have to fix it.

So Luke hooked up the hayrack and headed back out to the field to load up the critically injured pig. The pig must have weighed over 100 pounds, but somehow Luke was able to wrestle it to his shoulder and dump it onto the hayrack. He then drove around the corncrib and chose a burial site. It hadn't rained for weeks so the ground was as hard as concrete.

Luke got a pickax and a shovel from the tool shed and started digging. It was really tough going but he finally convinced himself that the hole was deep enough.

He went back to the tool shed to look for a big hammer for the euthanasia effort.

He was hoping that by this time the pig had died of natural causes, but had no such luck.

Luke gave the pig's forehead four or five of his hardest shots and feeling a little queasy, quickly got up on the rack and shoved the carcass into the hole. To his dismay, the hole was barely deep enough. It looked as if there would be only two or three inches of dirt covering the pig's body. There was no way Luke could ever get it out of the hole to dig deeper, so he grabbed the shovel and covered the body with dirt.

Luke looked at the loose dirt with a good deal of anguish and regret as there was a barely detectable rise and fall, rise and fall, rise and fall. It couldn't have lasted too long and Luke didn't stick around to see!

Farming was turning out to be a really tough job and in two days Luke had cost his employer quite a bit more than his $5 a day salary.

Working on a hog farm could be dangerous. When someone had to cross the hog lot to the feed bins, some of the big ornery sows tried to sink there teeth into his leg. Luke relayed to his boss his trepidation about handling this chore and the boss told him to just carry a five-gallon bucket with him as he crossed the pen. That sounded easy enough, so Luke picked up the magic bucket and walked semi-confidently across the pig lot. The biggest, meanest sow immediately charged and grabbed a mouthful of his pant leg. Luke dove over the fence and barely escaped. He was a little shaken and reported that the magic of carrying the bucket didn't seem to work. The part that his boss had left out was that as the sow charged you were supposed to smack him in the mouth with the bucket—an important piece of information that Luke should have had!

The breeding session for the pure-bred Spotted Poland China hogs was a real orgy. Not a lot of foreplay, but lots of grunting and squealing. Some of the boars serviced multiple partners and Luke was told that when help was needed he was to reach down and guide the boar's equipment to aim for penetration. This sounds pretty crude but it really wasn't so bad. Just think for a minute about how hard sex might be without hands and not being able to talk! This was definitely basic sex education without the moral implications!

Gathering eggs was another troublesome adventure. Luke was never too fond of birds of any kind. He would go as far as to say that he had a little bit of a hidden fear of touching any kind of a bird. Gathering 90 per cent of the eggs was a piece of cake, but there were always three or four obstinate hens that refused to move off the nest. No way was Luke going to reach under that hen to pull her off the nest to get the eggs. He tried poking with a stick, but the hen would just duck and squirm. If they wanted to keep those damn eggs that badly Luke was not that interested in the final count. The boss's wife expressed some concern that the output was down and Luke suspected that at the end of his three-week work stint there were a couple of nests that had maybe a dozen eggs well warmed.

There were some bright spots. Every farm meal was a feast and most were followed by a short nap before heading back to work. The farmer's daughter was about Luke's age and one of the prettiest girls in school and a couple of afternoons he was ordered to help her pick cherries. This was more like it!

When Luke's three week work stint was up the farmer told him that he had worked hard and done a good job, putting aside a dead hog and some plowed-out corn. He said that he was not going to say anything to Luke's dad or anybody about his "screw-ups." This is not the exact word he used but both he and Luke knew what he meant.

Luke gained a great appreciation of how hard farmers work in the summer and how varied and sometimes dangerous the work environment was. There were far too many reports of farmers losing fingers, thumbs or hands trying to unclog corn pickers. One little farm girl had her thumb torn off by a hay rope and on the way to the hospital she asked her dad if it would grow back. One unfortunate farmer was blinded when a gust of wind blew fertilizer in his eyes. Tractors tipped over on drivers, bulls gored their handlers and, of course, hogs tried to bite an inexperienced workers leg off.

It could be dangerous for the farm animals as well as for the farmer. (reference- Luke's pig killing episode) Luke had a friend whose dad farmed in the next county who was a pretty big drinker. One day this farmer and his hired man hit the bottle early in the afternoon and were pretty well lit when they went to pick up a few head of sheep in their truck. The farmer called the sheep his "lawn mowers." He would turn them loose in his barn lot and they would eat the grass to the point where he didn't have to mow. After picking up a half dozen sheep in the truck, they roared away heading for home. They decided to stop at the small town tavern for a happy hour drink and to show off the sheep to their beer-drinking buddies.

As they ushered their friends to the rear of the truck for a look, they discovered that both had thought the other had replaced the tail gate and along the fifteen mile trip to the bar they had lost all of the sheep.

This, of course, falls outside the hazards normally associated with farming.

Outdoor urination was pretty common on the farm. A farmer wouldn't, for example, drive to the house for this function, he would just hop off the tractor and pick a spot.

An inexperienced town kid Luke knew did this once while plowing for a local farmer. He picked a spot at the end of a corn row near the barbed wire fence. He didn't know that the fence was electric and urinated on it. Talk about hazards on the farm and picking the wrong spot. This is a mistake that is not repeated.

Luke would say that, like the farmers, the town kids were never really shy about just picking a spot. If they were playing outside of town, they would often have distance pissing contests for dimes. You squeezed it as tight and as long as possible and then let it go. It was easy to mark the distance in the dirt of a plowed field. A key element was how really bad you had to go.

In the winter time, one of Luke's good friends would try to write his name while peeing in the snow. He would broadcast "B - i - l - l - - C - o - l - - - b he was starting to lose steam — - - - u - - - - r —-, one letter short. "Damn," he said, "I'd have made it if I hadn't stopped to dot the i.

Some men would have no chance trying this—guys like Nomar Garciaparra or Engelburt Humperdinck.

In Luke's high school years the federal government became a big player in summer work opportunities. The federal corn storage laws created all kinds of work on existing corn bins and on the building of new ones.

Luke's first government job was scraping out the rotted corn from emptied bins and "tarring" the floor and first ring of the steel wall. This was one of the world's hottest and foulest smelling jobs. The night after his first day doing this job he almost died from a ruptured appendix. This was God's way of telling Luke that he was not to be involved in this hot and stinking job. Because of Luke's invalid and recuperating condition he was assigned to help a couple of older gentlemen measure and plot new bin sites. It took a near-death experience to force the change of assignments. Same pay!

Luke's best paying job when he was in high school was "hanging steel" with a work crew building new government corn bins. $3.20 @ hour/ $4.80 overtime was huge money in 1956, and there was a lot of overtime. Minimum wage back then must have been about $1.25 an hour, so Luke thought that he had cracked the big time. It was long days and hard work but what a payday. It didn't last long, though. The next summer the government got out of the bin-building business and it went back to the private sector. Luke and his friends were asked to do the same work for $1.25 an hour and no more for overtime. Their plan was for the workers to stay late regardless of baseball games or other evening plans for no added pay rate. This was the first and only time Luke was ever fired. They didn't like his critique of their fiscal policies concerning overtime pay.

Not all of the work that Luke did growing up was for pay. His mom was pretty strict about chores around the house and yard. Luke and his sister mowed and trimmed their yard and every Saturday morning helped with the house cleaning. They either ran the vacuum cleaner or dusted. Luke hated dusting sort of like he hated trimming. When he mowed or ran the vacuum there was a lot more evidence that he was accomplishing something.

Luke's family didn't have an automatic washing machine nor a dryer. His mom would wash their clothes, rinse them by hand and then run them through the ringer. Luke would often take clothespins and hang the clothes on the clotheslines outside. It was amazing how frozen stiff the blue jeans and Levis got in the winter, like a board.

Burning the trash was a regular duty, so every house had a couple of empty 50-gallon barrels positioned near the garden or the alley. Luke never minded this duty. Watching a fire burn in the evening, even if it was trash, was not that bad.

The worst ever duty was when Luke's parents decided to kill and pick chickens to put in their freezer. It goes back somewhat to Luke's dislike or fear of birds. They would have about two dozen live chickens in a crate. Luke's dad would wring all of their necks and Luke was to pick up a chicken by its claws and dip it in scalding water. In the meantime, there were headless chickens actually running and flopping around all over the yard with blood everywhere. The basis for the saying, "He was running around like a chicken with his head cut off" is real and disgusting. Just smelling the stinkin' wet feathers and having to pull out the feathers was as bad as it gets. Luke offered to do anything to get out of this chicken massacre. It made his skin crawl.

Chapter Seven

In the fall of the year there was a lot of leaf raking and that led to one of the "smells" of the small town. Everybody raked their leaves to the edge of the street and lit a match to them. At times it seemed as if the whole town was on fire, but Luke always felt that it was a good smell. He and his friends would ride their bikes through the burning leaves trying to out do one another with acts of bravery.

While on the subject of small town smells, Luke's house was right on the east edge of town and one of the farmers had a barn and hog lot just across the road. One of the foulest odors on the farm is pig manure. The pigs were normally only there in the summer and happily the prevailing wind was from the west. There were days, though, when it was still or the wind was from the east and the stench was overpowering.

Finally, Luke and a couple of his high school friends worked once for a farmer who was pouring concrete floors for corn bins. As the farmer pushed the wheelbarrow full of concrete up the planked incline to dump it into the forms, he would say, "Vroom, vroom, vroom, vroom," like he was a kid making tractor sounds on his tricycle, sort of a lip "splutter." This was funny to them because they knew of a high school basketball player who would run down the floor and do the same thing. He would verbally shift his gears as he speeded up and ran past another player.

Maybe it made him run faster!

Chapter 8

Luke's dad worked hard driving a gas truck. When the farmers were in the field, whether planting in the spring or harvesting in the fall, keeping up with the demand for gasoline and diesel fuel made for long days. Some farmers just told Luke's dad to keep their tanks filled and that was good. He would stop on his way to a delivery and top off gas tanks. Others would wait until they were down to their last tractor tank of gas before calling in an order. Some seemed to assume that they were the only customer and count on his dad dropping everything and coming right out with a load of gas.

This job required a lot of physical labor. His dad climbed on the truck to load the gas, he went up and down the ladder with the heavy hose to fill the tanks, and he also hand delivered 50 gallon barrels of motor oil. Often his days were 10 or 12 hours long. He then bounced along from farm to farm in his truck and hurried back to town to reload. It was hard work and it was a grind.

In the summer, the pressure was to keep up with the production demands of the farmers. In the winter, it was the pressure of making sure that no one ran out of furnace oil on a cold winter night.

The township snow removal crews did the best that they could on the rural roads, but during a winter storm it was hard for them to keep up with the drifting snow. The farm lanes were the responsibility of the farmer. Some farmers worked hard to keep them open, while others didn't. Luke's dad got stuck many times in farm lanes and barn lots.

When delivering gas, his dad was always able to back right up to the tank, so it was usually a short pull with the hose. On the inside of the back door of the truck was an antiquated device to keep track by fives the amount of gas delivered. This was used before the arrival of electric pumps and hoses, when he had to carry one five-gallon bucket of gas at a time up a ladder to dump into the tank. What a back breaking chore that must have been!

Furnace oil was a whole different ballgame. The truck would be parked as close as possible to the house, but it was often a long pull through deep snow drifts to get the hose to the tank. Sometimes he would pull the hose halfway, find a dry spot to put the nozzle down, and go back to the truck and pull again.

This was where Luke was valuable as a helper, even as a kid. Luke would start out with the hose and get part way to the tank and then his dad would grab a different spot on the hose and the two of them pulling together made it somewhat easier.

There were many times on cold winter evenings when Luke's family was eating dinner and the phone would ring. Someone who hadn't given his dad the word to keep the tank full had run out of furnace oil. His dad would always get the truck out and go out into the cold night and make the delivery.

At least a couple of times each winter, it often seemed to be a Sunday afternoon, someone would drive up and park in front of Luke's house in an old pick-up truck or an old car. The man would get out and would just sort of stand by his car and scrape the gravel with the toe of his boot. He would never come to the door.

Luke's dad would go out and talk to him. It was some farmer's hired man. He and his family would be living in a tenant house and they would be out of fuel for their stove and would have no money to pay. There was always the promise that they would come to settle up on payday. Some did, but many could never catch up with everyday needs to be able to pay.

Never, did Luke's dad ever turn anyone down. He heard his dad tell his mom that he wasn't going to have those little kids living in a cold house. Luke often wondered if the farmer who had hired the tenant felt any responsibility. I'm sure some did but, sadly, many didn't.

Chapter Eight

Farm dogs were also a hazard faced by Luke's dad. Almost every farm had at least one dog and a few of them were big and mean and were meant to be that way as watchdogs. As his dad would get out of his truck the dog would come bounding at him barking and baring it's fangs. If he could get the nozzle of the hose in his hand he would wait until the dog was right on him and then give the dog a shot of gasoline in the face. This really was effective.

In subsequent trips to that farm, as soon as the dog saw that big white gasoline truck coming he would tuck his tail between his legs and run around behind the house and hide.

Luke's house always smelled like gasoline. His dad would throw his dirty clothes in the basement where Luke's mom did the wash. Some days they reeked and the smell just hung around. Luke actually sort of liked the smell of gas and the family just got used to it.

Luke's mom also worked hard (almost all the mothers *worked* at home). The family had a ringer-type washing machine in the tiny basement and handling the gas and oil-stained work clothes was a major challenge. At the same time his mother had to keep up with clothes for three kids. With no dryer, the clothes were hung outside and then there was always a big load of ironing.

Luke's family very seldom ate out except at church or school potlucks. His mom was a good cook. Luke never saw a rare steak or a slice of rare roast beef until he was in college. His mom cooked them really well done and he would always pour on the catsup. Often now, he feels guilty when he asks for catsup for his steak.

It's not clear whether some of the things that Luke's family ate were a product of being frugal, but here are some of the foods he was served.

• Creamed eggs on toast which were hard boiled eggs cut up in some sort of milky cream sauce and served over toast. They had this delicacy a lot at lunch.

• Fried bologna sandwiches. The grease content in the bologna made the slices curl up like bacon and they ate them with mustard like a hot dog.

• Peanut butter and pickle sandwiches, which was a sweet pickle sliced long ways on a thick layer of peanut butter.

• Liver and onions fried crispy black. Luke ate this with mustard, early on to hide the taste of the liver and he just learned to like it that way.

• An open face mayonnaise sandwich, which was a piece of white bread spread with thick layer of Miracle Whip mayonnaise.

• Franco-American spaghetti. Luke ate this most every Saturday noon while he watched the Lone Ranger. The meal consisted of hard kernels of well-done hamburger with spaghetti noodles in a greasy orange sauce. Luke was overwhelmed when he ate his first real Italian spaghetti at Casella's, an Italian restaurant in Bloomington.

• Pumpkin pie with a topping of either maple syrup or grape jelly.

• Dip on Cake. That is what it was called, "dip." It was sort of brown sugar topping poured over a plain yellow cake.

• Mashed potatoes with a topping of burnt cheese on a split wiener, eaten with a lot of catsup.

Luke's mom also made the world's greatest pickled beets. They had a tangy bite to them and she would fill huge jars with them. It is not "normal" for kids to be wild about pickled beets but her kids and grandkids loved them.

On really special occasions, Luke's family would make ice cream. They had an old fashioned hand operated ice cream maker. The ice bucket around the stainless steel core was made of wood slats and the ingredients needed were cream, sugar and a little vanilla.

They would buy a block of ice and put it in a gunny sack. They would then crush the ice by beating on it with a sledgehammer or the side of an axe. The ice was then packed around the core and they sprinkled salt on it often to melt it enough to allow a smoother turn of the handle. They took turns turning and turning and turning the handle waiting for the ice cream to freeze. The harder it was to turn the handle, the closer they were to the best ice cream ever. When it was ready, it was a special treat to take a spoon and clean the paddles that had churned the ice cream.

Luke's family always made a big point that it tasted extra good because of the hard work they put into turning the handle by hand. However when one of their relatives gave them an electric ice cream maker as a gift and they never turned that handle again and it tasted just as good. A final touch was a homemade hot fudge sauce with a few chopped nuts.

As a kid Luke lived in fear of getting the mumps. It was a little bit not wanting to miss any basketball games, but also one of his school teammates had the mumps and they went down to his testicles. His friend said that they got as big as grapefruits. His description of the painful ordeal scared the heck out of Luke.

In any case, almost all of Luke's friends and his sisters had had the mumps at one time or another so Luke was always feeling his glands to check for swelling. One day someone told him that the way to check for mumps was to eat a dill pickle. If the pickle tasted rotten, you had the mumps. Luke kept a jar of dill pickles in the refrigerator and every morning after his paper route he took the mumps test by eating a dill pickle. Luke guessed the dill pickle test worked. They never tasted rotten and he never had the mumps.

Sometime about the third or fourth grade, the wealthy family in town got the first television set. It was, of course, black and white and the reception was really "snowy."

After school there was a Howdy Doody Show on and that was the first television show Luke ever saw.

Prizefighting was a bigger sport back then, with fighters like Sugar Ray Robinson, Jake LaMotta, Willie Pep and, of course, the heavyweight champion, Rocky Marciano. Joe Louis was attempting a comeback against Marciano and the fight was being telecast. The living room of the home with the only TV in town was packed for the fight. The picture was so snowy that viewers could vaguely see two bodies groping around the ring. Joe Louis, who many feel was the greatest heavyweight champion of all time, was far past his prime and was knocked out that night by Marciano. The next day at the tavern everybody who was there to see the fight on TV, was marveling at what a great fight it was, describing the punch that knocked Louis out. Really, if they hadn't been told that it was a boxing match being televised, they would have had a hard time figuring it out from the grainy quality of the picture.

Part of the reason for the "snowy" television reception was that the antenna had to be pointed precisely in the direction of the signal. In Luke's town that was to the southeast toward Champaign. There was no electrical gadget yet to reposition the antenna. The husband would get up on the roof with a big pipe wrench and manually turn the antenna a few inches and yell down to his wife "Is it better now, Wanda?" The wife would shrilly call back, "Not yet, Bill, keep turning!"

Steadily though, they moved into the television age with "Perry Mason, Ed Sullivan, I've Got a Secret, What's My Line, The Hit Parade, the Honeymooners, Gunsmoke and I Love Lucy" being the first wave of shows Luke would watch. Then came televised baseball, Dizzy Dean "he "*slud*" into third base" and Pee Wee Reese doing the Game of the Week (Hamm's Beer – from the "land of sky blue water!")

It was still a long way from one of the greatest technological advances in TV history, the remote control. In some homes it is called the U.P. —- the "Ultimate Power."

The radio shows like "Climax, the Lone Ranger, the Shadow, Fibber McGee and Molly and Jack Benny" were soon to be a thing of the past.

Luke stayed overnight once in a while with a friend who lived on a farm. At night when they milked the cows they had the barn radio tuned into Sergeant Preston and Yukon King.

It was amazing how every night each cow went to exactly the same stall. Don't you wonder what would have happened when a new cow joined the herd? Who then made the stall assignment and what happened if she unintentionally slipped into a veteran's slot? It was also amazing how it looked so easy to squeeze milk from a cow's teats and yet how hard it was. Luke's friend could shoot a stream all the way across the barn and hit a cat in the mouth and Luke couldn't get even a drip or two in the bucket.

When Luke was in grade school, for probably the first time ever the high school basketball team's game in the county tournament was broadcast on the radio. Someone recorded the game and many of the fans gathered in the Chrysler-Plymouth showroom to listen to the replay. Luke's school team had lost the game and still it was a big deal to be able to hear it on the radio. Luke remembers feeling sorry for the high school star who was there listening when the announcer criticized him for loafing. The star sort of chuckled and got up and left, but the comment hurt and embarrassed him.

The county tournament was a really big deal for the community and the grade school kids worshipped the high school athletes. They were the role models and set the tone, even for things such as hair styles. Flat top crew cuts were in vogue, and the school administrators were upset when a local barber cut the initial "O" (the first letter of the school's name) in some players' hair. Luke was not allowed by his parents to follow this lead.

The other major sports heroes were major league baseball players. Every summer Luke's dad would take him to Chicago to a Yankee/White Sox doubleheader. He will never forget his awe the first time that he saw the Comiskey Park baseball field.

The field was so big and so green. This was before television and Luke had heard the radio announcer talk about the "ball park," but in his mind he pictured a city park. It became his dream to be the shortstop for the Yankees. He was every bit as big as Phil Rizzuto.

In 1950 Luke had a difficult decision to make. As a White Sox mailing list subscriber, his dad had been able to buy four tickets to the major league All-Star game at Comiskey Park.

The game was scheduled at the same time that Luke was scheduled to go to 4-H camp.

Since camp was a four-day experience, the family decision was that Luke go to camp. This gave his dad a chance to take three farmer friends to the game. His dad, a Yankee fan, took two White Sox fans and a Cub fan and saw the National League win a 14 inning thriller on Red Schoendienst's home run. Their seats were in the upper deck deep in the left field corner and slightly behind a pole. It didn't really matter to them because they were there for maybe the best All-Star game of all time.

Luke had a great time at camp

Chapter 9

Luke's paternal grandparents had been tenant farmers before moving to town. He had a distant memory of riding on the back of the plow horses as his grandpa watered them at the end of a day's work in the fields. He was really young, maybe two years old, so there is a chance he doesn't remember as much as he recalls seeing a grainy old photo of this happening.

His grandparents farm home had no electricity and when at their home he was read to by the light of a kerosene lamp. Also, in the winter, his grandma would wrap a hot brick in some sort of towel and put it in the end of their bed for warmth. His grandma would also walk the roadside and pick "greens" which she would soak in vinegar as a part of their meal. She also walked the railroad tracks to pick wild strawberries, so tiny that it took forever to get enough for strawberry shortcake.

His grandma would sew soybeans in cloth bags for him. She would then cut the bottom out of a round oatmeal box

Grandma

and nail it above the door in the living room. This was Luke's first practice basketball hoop. It was beanbag basketball.

When his grandparents retired, they moved into a tiny one-bedroom house across the alley from where his family lived. They now had electricity, of course, and running water, but still had an outdoor toilet and his grandma cooked on a large coal stove. There was a shed near the alley where she kept some cobs and coal.

His grandma had a bad knee, which she wrapped regularly and she limped noticeably. Today, it is certain that she would be a candidate for a knee replacement.

Luke's grandfather used to love horseradish and he ate his peas with a knife. He smoked a cigar and had kind of a gruff demeanor. At this stage of his life, he was in poor health.

One winter night when Luke and his family were eating supper at his house, the back door was jerked open and his grandma stumbled in and sobbed, "Come quick, I think dad's gone."

Luke's dad knocked over a couple of chairs as he ran for the back door imploring Luke's mom to quick call the doctor. Luke was just in the third grade and this was the first really traumatic moment in his life.

Grandma was right, Luke's grandfather was dead. What a terrifying run that must have been for his grandma in the dark with her balky knee and the sadness of the news that she feared she was carrying.

Luke's first funeral ever was his grandpa's. It was very sad for him to see his dad and mom and grandma and aunts cry. The hymn that was sung was "The Old Rugged Cross," which was his grandma's favorite.

After his grandpa died, Luke's family spent lots of time helping grandma, mowing her yard and helping her with chores. She had a glass eye, which if the kids asked her to she would take out and show them. At one time or another Luke brought all of his friends by to see her glass eye.

Luke's grandma was really a kind and caring person. She started eating all of her evening meals at his family's house after his grandpa died and she always insisted that she be allowed to wash the dishes, wanting in this way "to pay something for her meal." This was okay with Luke, because it had been his and his older sister's job and now they just took turns drying the dishes.

Whenever Luke's family had fried chicken, his grandma always insisted that she liked the back, the neck, and the gizzard best. This was because she didn't want to take any of the prime pieces from others. Nobody could really like the back, the neck, and the gizzard best! The back had no meat on it at all and did you ever see a chicken neck?

People don't cut a chicken like they used to and they have pretty much eliminated the wishbone. Luke's family members would take turns "pulling" the wishbone to see who got the biggest half and the promise of good luck. If they had never ever cut up chicken the old fashioned way the Nebraska Cornhusker football team would have had to find a different name for their offense than the "Wishbone"

After the evening meal one or more of the kids always walked grandma home and made sure that she got the lights on in her house, with her telling them all the way that it wasn't necessary.

One day, she was walking across the railroad tracks from the store when she found a dead body. It was one of the men who worked at the grain elevator. She went to the elevator to get help. They couldn't move the body until the coroner arrived at the scene, so someone covered the body with a tarpaulin from one of the trucks. Luke's grandma went to her home and got a clean white sheet. She felt that it was disrespectful to see them cover the body with a corn tarp.

Luke never had too much of a relationship with his grandparents on his mother's side. His grandma died when his mom was a baby and his grandpa lived in Michigan and worked in an automobile plant. He would visit once in a while and Luke's mom was always excited that he was getting to see her children. When he visited was the only time that there was beer in the family's refrigerator and he was always eager to get to see his old buddies at the pool hall in the neighboring town.

A couple of Luke's friends had grandparents in town. One of his friends was from a really strong Republican family. In Luke's case, his dad felt that Franklin Delano Roosevelt was the greatest man of all-time, with Harry Truman a close second, so Luke was indoctrinated in that vein. He remembers being with his parents when they heard the announcement of FDR's death on their car radio. The car was parked in their drive near their garden with the radio on while his mom and dad and another couple were digging potatoes. When they heard the news tears came to their eyes.

Big Maw

Anyway, this Republican friend and Luke were working one day at the egg plant and they were, in a very uninformed way, arguing about politics. His friend's grandfather happened by and heard what they were talking about. He took his grandson's side, which Luke understood. Luke was jolted, though, when he told them that he could never vote for a Democrat because they had "killed my son." His son had died serving the country in World War II. Luke was embarrassed and didn't respond, but he went home and told his mom and dad what had been said. They just tried to make Luke understand how much a father loved his son.

There were a couple of other of Luke's friends whose grandmother and great-grandmother were called Mert and Big Maw. Mert was full of spice and loved doing things with the town's kids. She would dress up and go Halloweening with them. In those days the kids all went as one group and would go into the homes for their treats. Part of the deal was to have people guess who they all were. Mert always fooled them and got a big kick out of it.

Big Maw was about 4 feet 2 inches tall and about that wide. She didn't go out much but shuffled around the house pretty well on those short legs. Mert would have the kids put a few bales of hay in the back of a pick-up truck. They would lift Big Maw in with the kids and then drive into the country and park. Sometimes they would stop in an open field and Mert would point out the important stars, sometimes they would park in the cemetery and she would tell ghost stories and once in a while they would go to a part of a neighboring village that Mert called "skunk town." This was where the poor families of the coal miners had lived and she had stories about the coal miners.

Besides the grandparents, there were quite a number of older people living in Luke's town including many older widows. Everyone in town sort of looked after each other and special attention was given to these ladies. The church in town was very important to these older folk.

Luke's family was a church-going family. Everyone dressed up for church, the men all wore suits and ties, the women their very best dresses and the kids wore their "Sunday school clothes." The importance of another event could sometimes be rated by whether Luke and his sisters were told to wear their Sunday school clothes. It was pretty much a two hour commitment every Sunday morning. Young children went to the basement to color Bible pictures and play in the sandbox and everyone else went to an age group Bible lesson.

Crunch time was when Luke asked his mom and dad if he had to stay for church. He seldom ever got a pass to skip church.

Their minister was a fire-and-brimstone orator. He would loudly and with a flourish warn of the evils of sin, and then pull his handkerchief from his pocket, slowly wipe the sweat from his forehead and the saliva from his chin and mouth and then almost conspiratorially whisper the good news of Jesus.

The church didn't offer communion every Sunday. About once every two months they would have "Communion Sunday." The entire congregation would line up across the front of the church and down all of the aisles. One server would pass out tiny squares of white bread which the people would hold in their hands until the wine had been handed out. In the summer with no air conditioning in the church and a sweaty palm, the bread got a little soggy. Each person was then handed a tiny shot glass of wine. The minister would identify the bread as the body of Christ and everyone would eat. He would then identify the wine as the blood of Christ and everybody would drink. The ceremony took a good bit of time.

One really hot summer Sunday, an older lady fainted and fell over a low wall that that ran along a side aisle. She did almost a head stand and her feet stuck straight up in the air with her dress around her waist. Her heavy hose were rolled to just below her knees.

Luke and his friends knew that it wasn't funny. Thankfully, she was not injured.

The church never had air conditioning, so almost everyone used a handheld fan. The cardboard fan had a wooden handle and on one side of the fan was a religious picture and on the other side was an advertisement for a funeral home.

At some point Luke became a member of the choir. His alto would have been accurately described as a monotone. The seat in the back row did give him a good look out a window to see if there was any rain in sight to threaten that afternoon's baseball doubleheader.

The church was small and once at a funeral all of the kids in town tried to squeeze into the same pew. One of the girls whispered for everybody to scoot over, she said that she was sitting on a crack. One of the guys whispered back, "Aren't we all." They couldn't stop giggling which was totally inappropriate and the result of this was some parental discipline when the kids got home.

With or without the church's involvement, the town sort of looked out for it's own.

There were two people in town who today would be known as mentally challenged.

It seemed as if every small town had someone who would fit this description, often unkindly referred to as the "village idiot." Luke's town had two. Most times they were able to lead productive lives and in some ways they were also looked after by the townspeople.

No one really seemed to know exactly how old Harry was or what had happened to his mother, as she was never around. Harry was probably in his 50s when Luke was a kid.

He lived with his father, who was a carpenter. The house that they lived in reminded Luke a lot of Boo Radley's house in the movie "To Kill a Mockingbird."

Both Harry and Boo Radley would be identified as retarded, but Harry was no Boo Radley. He didn't seem to have a kind side and most of the kids were a little afraid of him. It is certain that after dark when they rode by his house on their bikes they sped up. The house was always very dark, almost as if the only lighting provided was a couple of bare 30 watt light bulbs hanging from the ceiling.

Harry spent a lot of time mowing his yard with an old fashioned push mower. He was a little bit of a hunchback, he always wore bib overalls and he walked up and down the sidewalk in front of his house with his hands in his pockets.

For some reason he would get really angry if anyone called him Henry Clay. Of course, when the kids in town found this out they would ride by on their bikes and holler "Hey Henry Clay." He would shake his fist and mutter angrily in response. It is really a mystery why being called Henry Clay would bother him so much. It would be interesting to know the story behind this, or how he even knew anything about Henry Clay.

Old timers remember that he played the accordion and rode around town on a girl's bike. Luke never saw that side of Harry.

Charles Ray, on the other hand, went through grade school with the kids and lived all of his life in the town. He must have started school at a later age, because he was eight years older than Luke was. He suffered from epileptic seizures and it was scary how strong he was as teachers tried to hold him down to keep him from hurting himself during a seizure. There was the great fear that he would swallow his tongue.

He was an easy target for kids to tease. The thing that would agitate Charles Ray the most was someone telling him that they were the teacher's pet. He would get all red faced and say "No you're not the teacher's pet, I am."

Charles Ray had a mother and dad and a couple of sisters. His dad was a farm hand for the town founder's farm so he drove a tractor around town a lot. He had a loud voice which could be heard blocks away and had the bluest vocabulary imaginable.

When Charles Ray rode his bike, he would roll one pant leg up so that it would not get caught in the chain. He would ride on the dirt or gravel roads so he could look back constantly to see how much dust he was making.

Church was a big part of his life and he treasured being the person who rang the church bell calling people to worship. He would pull that rope with an extra effort and churchgoers would praise him for doing a good job. He relished the responsibility he had for mowing the churchyard. He took the garbage out for the local tavern, and when this business was sold, his job was a part of the package.

Charles Ray was not allowed to go to high school. No one ever knew how they explained this to him. He had a little of Boo Radley's kindness in him, particularly as he got older. He became really involved in the church and was looked after by the whole town.

The townspeople, then, were an interesting mix with a little tilt to older folk. Of course in those days when you turned sixty it seemed as if you were considered "old."

Everyone in town knew much about everyone else, even a whole lot about their pets.

Chapter 10

There were no leash laws for the dogs in Luke's town. Townspeople never had a license for their dogs and some would wander all over town. Daisy Mae, their dog, always stayed pretty close to home. Daisy Mae was a white long-haired dog with a splash of rust and black on her chest. She was a mix of many breeds.

Their bachelor neighbor had a girlfriend who lived with him for a while. Her name also happened to be Daisy Mae. He had outdoor plumbing (an outhouse), so that for bathroom functions they had to walk down a long board path to the alley.

When the girlfriend would walk down there, as she would inevitably have to do, Luke and his friends would get great fun out of whistling and calling the dog. "Here Daisy Mae, Here Daisy Mae, come on girl!" They laughed and giggled and really felt that they were being cute.

If a dog that was supposed to be a stay-at-home dog wandered to another part of town, someone almost certainly would scold him and tell him to go home. "Skippy Orr, you get home!" That was another thing, most of the dogs in the town had last names. There was Skippy Orr as well as Spotty Abell and Dopey Meiners to name a few. All of these dogs were mixed-breed.

The grade school principal and coach bought a purebred female German Shepherd with a plan to breed her and sell the pups as a money-making scheme. The German Shepherd escaped her pen one night and ran into Dopey Meiners. The result was a litter of 12 pups that looked a lot more like Dopey than like their purebred mother.

Luke's family never took long family vacations because his dad could not be away from his job for long periods. If the family went to Indiana for a weekend they never worried about boarding Daisy Mae. They knew that there were no garbage disposals in town and enough people dumped their garbage in the ditches that Daisy Mae would make out all right.

One time they were gone for a couple of days and forgot to let the dog out before they left. When they returned she had left her mess on the floor in front of the toilet stool. She knew where it was, she just didn't have the skills to execute.

One time Daisy Mae came home with what they all thought were a couple of dead rats and they were heaping praise on her for being such a great hunter. Later that morning they discovered that they were really very young kittens with no fur from a litter of a neighbor's cat. Daisy Mae was confused as to how she went from hero to bum in the matter of a few hours.

The only dog in town that everybody was kind of afraid of was Rex. Rex was a big Black Labrador that was a guard dog for the egg candling plant. No one knew of anybody who was bitten by Rex, but if anyone got anywhere near the egg plant they were faced with a menacing growl.

One morning when Luke was delivering papers, Rex and Scottie Molck, a little black Scottish Terrier were having an amorous moment right in the middle of the tavern corner which is the main intersection in town. Sort of like State and Madison in Chicago. It is doubtful, though, that you would have an opportunity to see this kind of action at State and Madison. All of the farmers gathered there for their morning coffee were laughing at the dramatic difference in the size of the dogs. There could be some anatomical term for it, but Rex and Scottie "got locked up," they couldn't end the encounter. Cars and pickup trucks were honking and swerving around to miss them. Even a huge Harvester combine had to maneuver to avoid interrupting the moment. The one liners from the farmers you might classify as "barnyard." Finally one of the farmers went into the tavern and got a bucket of cold water and threw it on them which evidently relaxed one or the other of them and they broke apart. Luke remembers how crude the comments being made by the men on the tavern corner were.

Chapter Ten

Seldom was there a dog fight, but if there was, it was scary. If it happened to be a fight between dogs in Luke's circle of friends, they all jumped in to separate the dogs, and then pointed the finger of blame squarely on the other guy's dog.

In the summer they would have Daisy Mae shaved and she seemed embarrassed. She skulked around with her tail between her legs and everyone felt sorry for her.

As she got older she went deaf and partially blind. Luke's family resisted even talking about having her put to sleep, but one day she was sleeping in the shade under their car and didn't hear the car start. She was run over and injured and Luke's dad took her to the vet to be put to sleep. They ultimately got another nice dog named Jodie. Jodie was a red-haired something. They loved her, but not quite like Daisy Mae.

Chapter 11

In those days it seemed that there was a lot of local controversy about which was the better automobile, Ford or Chevy? Once in a while Plymouth was in the mix, but only because there was a Chrysler-Plymouth dealership in town.   It was kind of a family thing really, you were either a Ford family or a Chevy family and the arguments over appearance, speed and performance were unending.

There was a lot of secrecy involved when the new model cars were to be introduced. There were dramatically fewer models back then, so every car was easily identified.

"Have you seen the new Oldsmobile?   Wow is it sharp." Ford, Chevy, Plymouth, Chrysler, Oldsmobile, Buick, Mercury and Pontiac pretty much covered it.   There were a few Dodges, DeSotos and Studebakers also around. Now there are so many foreign and domestic makes and models and no real common release date so the new-car excitement is not such a big deal.

Actually, for a really short period of time there was a Kaiser-Frazer dealership in town. The Kaiser and Frazer were possibly the ugliest looking cars ever built. Their big selling point was the first push-button door openers and they may have introduced the first electric windows. This was touted as the car of the future, but it looked a lot like a bloated boat.

The first car that Luke owned personally was a 1937 Chevy. It was about 17 years old when he bought it for $75. It had a long-handled gear shift on the floor. The car had sort of a fuzzy cloth seat and the right front fender was somewhat mangled. Luke was given about a 15 mile radius in which he could travel with this vehicle, sort of like the invisible perimeter fence that city people have for their dogs. If the dog goes over the perimeter wire it gets zapped. If Luke went over the perimeter and his mom found out, he got zapped.

Gas back then was about 30 cents a gallon. It was very common to pull into a gas station—a lot of people back then called them filling stations, and ask for a "buck's" worth. Of course he would ask the attendant to wash the windshield. Sometimes when Luke and his friends were heading out of town, they would pool their nickels, dimes and quarters until they came up with a dollar for gas. Today a dollar will get you less than a half-gallon and if you want your window washed you wash it yourself.

One night Luke was coming home from a date on a rural gravel road. He was missing curfew so he was driving faster than he should have when suddenly he was in the middle of a herd of black angus cattle. They were everywhere, in the ditch and on the road. Luke weaved in and out and missed many of them but finally banged one right in it's rear. She discharged manure all over the side of his car, but luckily just further damaged the mangled fender.

When Luke got home he rinsed the cow manure off with a bucket of water. Since the only damage was the already dented fender, he said nothing about the collision. Luke waited anxiously for a few days for word of a dead or injured cow, but none was forthcoming. It seems that he just scared the shit out of her!

Luke owned this gem for about two years and then sold it to a classmate for $175. About a month after the sale, the front axle broke. Luke felt bad, but….

His second car was his all-time favorite. It was a black 1950 Ford. The 1950 Ford was the one with the pointed ball in the middle of the grill. It was a "stick shift," which was pretty standard at that time. Automatic transmissions were first offered in cars in around 1948.

There was a man in town who had a slight speech defect. When automatic transmissions were introduced, he said he could never drive a car without a "crutch." Most of the high school kids agreed, to "peel out" or for short drag racing you definitely needed to pop the clutch.

When these Fords first came out they were so popular that one of the "time passers" on family trips was a contest to count the 1950 Fords you saw

Luke's Ford had belonged to an older high school kid and Luke had coveted it for a long time. He bought it in 1956 so it was not a really old car. It had dual exhaust with mufflers that sort of purred. It had fender skirts on the rear with wide white sidewall tires and the back end rode really low. It was one of the first cars that had rear speakers and of course the steering wheel had a "spinner" so that Luke could turn corners more easily with one hand.

He wouldn't have traded it for even the new cars that a couple of other kids owned.

Luke's family was a Ford family. Actually, they never once bought a new family car. There was a farmer who lived in town whose son-in-law owned a Ford dealership in a neighboring town. He bought a new Ford every year and really took good care of it. He smoked a cigar, but the cigar smell never seemed to be an issue. Every other year when this farmer traded cars, Luke's dad traded for the one he traded in. In the "hot" years, Luke was always really excited to see what car the farmer bought, because he knew in two years it would be his family's. The car purchased in 1956, was especially memorable because the guy bought a two-tone tan and beige Fairlane. It had the chrome down the side that sort of formed a V on the front door. Luke could hardly wait for 1958, when it would be his family's car.

Luke's and his family took really good care of their cars. They washed them often and for a good number of years had no hose so that after washing with soap and water they would have to carry buckets of water from the house to rinse.

A lot of the farm kids were good mechanics. Luke never really got too interested in the automobile engine. He knew where the distributor cap was, he knew what a spark plug looked like and he could locate the carburetor. Having any idea how they functioned or how to adjust or repair them was foreign to him.

He could change the oil. He would drive his car astride the shallow ditch in front of the gasoline bulk plant. He would then crawl in the ditch under the car and take the plug out of the oil pan and empty the old oil into a can. This old oil was then poured on the gravel drive to help keep down the dust. Luke would then replace the plug, being careful to not tighten it too tight and strip the threads. Finally he poured in four quarts of oil—five if he changed the filter. He was actually pretty proud of this minor automotive accomplishment.

Luke could change a tire, too. At least he thought he could. The first time he changed one on his own he failed to replace the lug nuts bevel side in and the car wobbled all the way home. His dad quickly corrected him. With the used tires and re-treads he put on his car, Luke had lots of opportunities to practice changing tires.

Luke also had an old bumper jack that raised the frame of the car about waist high before getting the tire high enough to replace. The down mechanism on the jack wouldn't work so when he had the spare tire mounted, he simply had to step back and kick the car off the jack. He didn't claim any style points, but he got the job done.

Chevy introduced a fuel injection engine in 1956. A friend of Luke's drove one of these Chevys. Once in awhile they would race the last four miles home from a date. Luke would never admit it, but the Ford couldn't keep up. That didn't end the Ford-Chevy argument, car loyalty was a big thing.

Chapter 12

About the only big city Luke ever visited was Chicago and except for his newspaper carrier trip there, his impressions of the city were of the south side area around Comiskey Park. His parents took him every year to a Yankee-White Sox doubleheader. They took the brick-paved Halstead Street by the stockyards into the mostly racially segregated neighborhood around the ball park. The relative poverty of this area was the image Luke had of what a big city was like for a long time.

Luke and a good buddy of his did have one other big city adventure the summer after his sophomore year in high school. It was a spur of the moment decision with absolutely no planning and Luke now has a hard time believing that the parents agreed to let the two of them go.

The two friends were playing on opposing teams in a Sunday afternoon baseball game. The friend was 17 years old, two years ahead of Luke in school. Luke was playing shortstop and in an early inning, his friend was a base runner on second base.

Chapter Twelve

Luke asked the friend if he was working the next week and he answered that he wasn't. Neither was Luke so he suggested that they take a trip. Since Luke was a big Yankee fan he knew that the Yankees were playing the Cleveland Indians a four-game series in New York at the end of the next week. Luke suggested that they ask their parents if they could drive to New York for the games. They decided that they both could come up with $50 from bin-building jobs to finance the trip. It is unclear how they decided that $50 would be enough, but $50 back then was quite a bit of money. They would have to pay for gas, lodging, food and game tickets. They had no plan for what to do if they ran out of money—in those days there were no credit cards or ATM's to fall back on. They evidently never even considered that they might not be able to buy tickets for such a big series between the Indians and the Yankees, who were in a dead heat for the American League lead.

Luke's buddy said that he would ask his parents and if they said yes he would pick Luke up at his home after the game. The game went 15 innings and it was almost dark when the kid drove up in front of Luke's house. Luke was worn out from the long game and was lying on the front porch swing. He had completely forgotten the conversation about New York.

The buddy said, "Are you ready to go?" Luke said, "Heck, I haven't even asked mom and dad if I can go." So he went into the house and calmly told his parents that he and his friend wanted to drive to New York to watch the Yankees and Cleveland play.

Luke doesn't remember a lot of "what if" conversation except the parents asked if they had any money. Luke's dad knew that his friend's Chevy burned a little oil, so he went to the bulk plant and gave them a case of oil. Luke quickly packed a couple of pairs of Levis and T-shirts and they were heading for the Big Apple.

They headed east on Route 165 and actually stopped at a girl's farm home near the next town about eight miles from home. They had heard that she was having a party, so they stopped to see "what was happening." They stayed a couple of hours, and as everybody was leaving they announced that they were headed for New York City. The reaction was "Yeah, right."

Luke was 16 years old and had just had his driver's license about four and a half months. The 1948 Chevy his friend had was a stick shift and Luke was used to driving an automatic transmission (he had passed his driver's test in a car with automatic transmission), but he had some experience with a clutch while driving a tractor working his farm jobs.

They had to know about the Pennsylvania Turnpike but maybe they were worried about the traffic—or maybe they didn't want to spend money on tolls—but for whatever reason they went two lane highways all the way.

Luke had a lot of trouble in towns on hills because he hadn't mastered holding the car on a hill with the clutch partially depressed at a stop light. When the light changed he had to make the quick move from the brake to the accelerator as he released the clutch and took off. He got better at it the farther they went.

At some point they looked at a map and decided to stop in Washington D.C. on their way because the Yankee/ Cleveland series didn't start until Friday. They figured they would have a little extra time so why not.

They slept in the car that first night for a few hours and a state patrolman rapped on their window to tell them that they had forgot to turn out their lights as they slept in a gas station parking lot.

Traveling through the Mountains of West Virginia on blacktop roads Luke was using the brakes to control speed downhill rather that down-shifting. As their car rolled into a small town, the brakes failed completely. They were able to turn onto a side street and stop. At that time there were mechanics working at almost all gas stations and they were able to get brake work done by an all-night mechanic, but it put a dent in their funds.

Meals were mostly roadside baloney or peanut butter and jelly sandwiches. They slept in the car. The cost of gas was about 30 cents a gallon. The case of oil would barely hold out for the trip.

It took them about 36 hours to get to D.C. They pulled in late at night and again slept in the car. When they awoke on their first morning in the nation's capital they were parked next to the Lincoln Memorial.

Luke's NY trip buddy.

The one day in D.C. was spent looking at the Capitol Building, the White House, and the monuments. Luke and his buddy never went inside any of the sites. That night they headed north to New York City, slept a couple of hours near the Holland Tunnel and entered the city with the early morning traffic through the tunnel. If Luke looked at a map today, he would be surprised to see that the Holland tunnel enters the city in

Greenwich Village near the tip of Manhattan. At the time, Luke and his friend had no idea exactly where they were except that they were in New York City.

They stopped at the first neon sign that said "Hotel." It was a small hotel and most certainly really cheap. They parked the car, checked in and asked how to get to Yankee Stadium, then followed the directions and took the subway to the Bronx to the "House that Babe Ruth built."

The date was, July 31, 1955, because that was the date that Sal Maglie, a New York Giant legend pitcher was claimed on waivers by Cleveland and joined the Indians that day in New York.

They were at the ball park when the gates opened and sat in the front row of the bleacher seats in right field. The outfield wall then was only about three feet high so they were really close to the field.

For baseball buffs, in that series Cleveland pitched Bob Lemon, Mike Garcia, Early Wynn and a rookie named Herb Score. The Yankees pitched Allie Reynolds, Vic Raschi, Ed Lopat and Whitey Ford. All are pitching legends for both of these teams.

The bad news for Luke, a Yankee fan, was that Cleveland swept the four game series.

The Yankees went on to win the American League pennant before losing to Brooklyn in the World Series, but it was a big disappointment for Luke to not get to see his team win at least one game.

The Cleveland pitchers were doing their pre-game running in the outfield right in front of where Luke and his friend were sitting. Some young fan kept yelling at Early Wynn. "Early, Early, Early Wynn, hey Early, Early, Early" —- and on and on. Finally Wynn, who was known for his temper turned and shouted "What, what, what man what?" Luke was wide-eyed.

All of the New York fans were trying to talk to Maglie, an arch enemy from his days with the Giants. They were worried that he was going to give the Indians a big lift in the pennant race against the Yankees.

The stay in New York consisted of three trips to Yankee Stadium, and they sat in about the same seats every day for two single games and a doubleheader. Luke doesn't remember wondering about or ever even talking about going to Times Square, or the Empire State Building, or the Statue of Liberty. After the games they would go to a grocery store and then eat in their room. They may have been afraid of going out on the town. They wouldn't have known where to go anyway and their funds were limited.

They made it home safely. Actually, they stopped in a town about 45 miles from home to get a half tank of gas to make it home and had enough money left to share a fried chicken dinner.

A couple of young high school kids from one of the smallest towns in the country on their own in the biggest city in the world, there to watch some baseball games.

Chapter 13

Halloween was a major event in Luke's small town. All grades at the school dressed in costumes and paraded from the school up the hill to the business district. It was a half-mile trek with many spectators out to watch.

One year Luke wore a Harry Truman mask, had on a double breasted-suit coat and chomped on a real cigar, which was left in the cellophane wrapper. Luke felt that he was doing something daring with the cigar and he won the prize for originality.

Halloween night all the kids in town would trick or treat at every house in town. As Luke and his friends got a little older, the trick or treat routine seemed a little tame. So one year they scattered and upended large stacks of used rubber tires, oil and lube signs, benches and picnic tables which created a mess on Main Street. As Luke delivered papers the morning after he and his friends' Halloween spree, he planted the word around that some kids from the neighboring town of Chenoa had been spotted in town. This news spread like wildfire, which fueled indignation and fooled most people in town. Luke and his friends, of course, vowed to make Chenoa pay in football.

Then, there was the tradition of that era of tipping over outhouses. The late 1940s was about the time in the town for a gradual transition to inside plumbing. What a step forward it was! In the winter it was so cold out that it was a huge decision whether to make a last trip outside before bedtime. Sometimes men just settled for a step out the back door. In summer, even though lime was sprinkled regularly in the outhouse, the odor and flies were sometimes overwhelming.

It was considered by some a celebration of Halloween to tip these outdoor "Johns" onto their backs. It was really not all that destructive, unless it fell hard enough to splinter the edge of the roof. Otherwise it was simply a case of getting some help to tip the small building back up over the hole.

Luke and his friends had a big scare once when they tipped one over on its front, not realizing that there was someone inside. This, of course, made it land on the door. Strategically then there were only a couple of small holes where a person could exit. They could tell by the yelling and what was being said that the user was not injured and they heard the next day that his yelling attracted help and he didn't have to use one of the round escape hatches.

It seemed a good idea one Halloween to throw water balloons at the principal's home.

Chapter Thirteen

It just happened that the balloons were red. The principal's wife deduced that Luke was one of the throwers involved (there were only five boys in town) and she called Luke's mom. She told her that the kids were throwing tomatoes at her house. Luke and his friends felt picked on by her accusations. Anyone could tell that balloon skins were not smashed tomatoes. They were insulted that she would accuse them of such a dirty deed. Luke's mom wanted to know why they thought it was okay to throw anything at someone's house and it ended with the kids' personal "heartfelt apology."

The townspeople back then pretty much accepted all of this as a part of the season, a part of kids growing up. Today the word they probably would use is vandalism.

Around Halloween time, hayrack rides were really popular. A tractor was used to pull a hayrack, with bales of straw placed strategically as seats and loose straw on the floor to keep the kids' feet warm (actually, a case could be made to call it a strawrack ride). The kids would climb aboard and sing and laugh as they traveled through the countryside.

Luke was in the seventh or eighth grade when he went to a party that included a hayrack ride. He was sitting with some buddies on the front of the rack and they were loudly proclaiming that the driver was driving to slow. They happened to be on the concrete highway (the hard road) leading to the neighboring town. Luke stood up on the tongue of the wagon, holding on as he turned to join the chorus of those clamoring for more speed.

He said, "Hey, I could run this fast" and one of his buddies gave him a friendly nudge and said, "Why don't you?" Luke lost his balance and started to fall. He was able to grab the front of the rack and hang on for a few seconds—maybe it was just a fraction of a second—while his friends frantically tried to pull him back up. His heels were dragging on the pavement and he couldn't hang on and he was swept under the hayrack.

The front wheels of the rack missed him, but with a big THUMP, the rear wheels of this heavily loaded rack ran over his legs around the thighs. Usually when there is a hayrack ride there are a number of hangers on following in cars and kibitzing. Luke is probably alive because on this night they were not.

When the other riders finally got the driver's attention and the tractor stopped, everybody rushed back to Luke's aid. He had cuts, scrapes and bruises all over his body and his legs felt numb.

When an injury occurs at a football game, the victim is not moved until they carefully strap him to a board. It was a different story this night because when they found that Luke was alive and conscious, they picked him up and put him in the backseat of a car that they hailed and took him to the local doctor. The doc bandaged his wounds and applied some stinging iodine to the scrapes. He gave Luke some pain pills and sent him home in the back seat of the family car.

Luke never had a stitch nor an X-ray. He was really sore for a couple of weeks, but luckily escaped with his life and no major injury.

Luke went on subsequent hayrack rides, but became smarter and always sat with a girlfriend near the middle of the rack.

With nothing to do in a small town, sometimes Luke and his friends would extend "Halloweening" acts to other months, and they had a slightly older high school mentor who would dream up stunts and talk them into pulling them off. Somehow, the mentor never put himself in jeopardy!

One sub-zero January night, the mentor had them raid the local county maintenance yard and "borrow" a couple of warning oil lamps and a couple of road signs. One road sign said "Highway Closed" and the other said "Heat Crack." They set this equipment up on the highway leading to the bridge over the Mackinaw River. They then hid in the road-side cemetery and watched as a half dozen cars stopped and turned around to find an alternate route around the bridge. Finally a local law officer showed up, got out of his car and gingerly walked to the middle of the bridge to check out the "heat crack." Sometimes they really had to search for entertainment!

Another time, the mentor was working a summer job at the old high school in Colfax.. The building had been converted into the junior high school. They rang the school bell every morning to signal the start of the school day. The mentor estimated that this bell had been calling kids to the start of school for an ungodly long number of years. He looked into his crystal ball and imagined for Luke and his friends how stunned the principal would be if when someone pulled the bell rope, nothing happened.

The charge then was to steal the clapper out of the bell. His plan involved leaving a lower level window unlocked when he left work. He made the point that it wasn't breaking and entering if you didn't "break" into the building. He drew up a floor plan indicating how to get to the belfry and listed the tools that would be needed and warned that after reaching the attic they must be careful to walk on the ceiling rafters so as to not step through a classroom ceiling.

The plan was perfectly executed, though they were lucky they didn't drop the clapper and have it fall through a ceiling. It weighed about 40 pounds.

The next morning they waited to "not hear" the bell ring. The silence was a private triumph. The administration acted quickly and that day went four miles to the school in Luke's town and took a clapper from a bell that was no longer in use. With the replacement clapper in place, only one day went by without a ringing bell. It was a small victory, but mission accomplished.

They hid the clapper at a friend's neighbor's farm. At some point one of the bell liberators panicked and wanted to get rid of the evidence. The story is that he threw it in the Mackinaw River. The legend of the bell clapper disappearance thus ended with only speculation and suspicion as to who was involved.

Another common prank was stealing watermelons, which became almost like a fall sport. There were a few farmers who raised watermelon, some probably just to provide a target for the kids. The watermelons in the stores were always a rich looking dark green on the outside and dark red and juicy on the inside. The locally-raised melons were usually a sickly looking yellow and not that tasty, so Luke and his buddies weren't stealing them to eat, but simply for the thrill of the hunt.

First the watermelon patch had to be located. Then a plan needed to be put in place to crawl through adjacent fields to get in position for the grab. Then, a getaway car had to be stashed at a safe location. It added to the excitement if the owner was alerted and defended his patch. A shotgun blast with the accompanying bird shot hitting the cornstalks made it a big time event.

There is no record of Luke or anyone ever getting caught or seriously injured. The grubby little melons tasted good only because of the effort involved.

Life wasn't all school, sports and pranks. Living in a small town did not shield kids from having to worry some about the troubles of the world. In their young lives their country was frequently involved in military conflicts around the world.

The atomic bomb was dropped on Hiroshima and Nagasaki in 1945 when Luke was six years old. This happened a few weeks before he started the first grade. President Harry Truman had been in office only a few months when he ordered the dropping of the first nuclear bomb. He was re-elected in 1948, defeating Thomas Dewey in a close election.

We were soon back in war in Korea in 1950 as North Korea attacked South Korea. The Korean armistice was signed in 1953 with Korea still divided at the 38th parallel. This was the summer after Luke's eighth-grade year.

Even as Luke and his friends started high school, the military draft was a possible factor in their future. He and his friends did not consider themselves unpatriotic, but none of them were really interested in serving in the Army.

A military recruiter came to their high school when they were sophomores. All of the boys in the school were called to an assembly in the gymnasium, where the recruiter explained to them that they had an eight-year military obligation.

He said that they could enlist in any branch of the service—Army, Navy, Air Force or Marines—which involved four years of active duty and four years in the reserves.

Another option was to wait to be drafted in the Army which would almost surely happen, and that would consist of a two year obligation of active service and six years in the reserves. The Army was the only branch of service that had a draft. He told them they could take advantage of a special window now and volunteer for the draft and choose any branch of service. This would be two years of active duty beginning soon after graduation with six years in the reserves. The lure of the special draft was to avoid the Army and get only two years active duty in the Navy or Air Force.   Finally, he said they could join the National Guard which involved a weekly one day meeting for eight years along with a two-week camp every summer.

Some of the seniors volunteered for the draft in the Navy and some guys in Luke's class decided to join the National Guard.

As the students were walking out a couple of Luke's younger friends asked him, "Hey, what are we going to do?" Luke said, "Nuthin, we are going to do nuthin." At that young age he didn't even want to think about being a soldier. For any of these kids at 15 years of age going into the military was really a heavy decision.   Luke felt that things change and maybe down the road the options would be different.

It worked out that going to college and then going into teaching and then having a child produced the deferments that kept Luke out of the military. If later in life he had decided to run for president he would have had to explain how he escaped the draft. It certainly wasn't preferential treatment, it was timing—or blind luck.

Chapter 14

A big focus of Luke's high school class was raising money for its senior trip. For four years the kids sold candy, washed cars, picked up corn, held used paper and scrap metal drives and conducted various other money making projects.

Graduation night, they used these funds to travel about 350 miles in a school bus to the Lake of the Ozarks for one last class party and chance to say good-bye. They survived a first-night crisis that had something to do with some boys trying to sleep in the girls' cabin. The faculty sponsors came within a hair of packing them up on the bus and sending them home, but cooler heads were able to work out a second chance based on a promise of good behavior.

The kids swam, went horseback riding, went boating, did the limbo with some kids from Oklahoma and enjoyed campfire meals.

One of Luke and his friends' big discoveries on the trip was that a girl in their class didn't shave her legs or underarms. It

was amazing how that could escape detection for four years—
a brunette at that.

The two love songs heard most at the campfire were Pat
Boone's "Love Letters in the Sand" and Elvis Presley's "Love
Me Tender."

This generation of graduates was heading for college at a
greater rate than their parents.

Three of Luke's classmates' mothers who were school
teachers were college graduates. There were no college grad-
uate fathers. Luke would be the first member of his family to
attend college. Seven or eight of his classmates were headed
to college, all boys and most were the first in their family to go
to college.

When the bus got home everyone scattered their separate
ways to begin the next step in their lives.

Chapter 15

The demographics of Luke's town have changed very little in about 60 years. The 2005 population is now 180, surprisingly it is up about 40 people. There are only ten people living in town now that were living there in the fifties. Four or five houses have been torn down, at least a half dozen houses are unoccupied and maybe a dozen new ones have been added. This is a net gain of about a half dozen homes in 60 years. Urban sprawl is not a problem there.

In many ways, in the sixty years since Luke grew up there this small town has changed dramatically. Most families now lock their homes, although a few still don't.

The business district is gone and there is no commerce except for the bank. At least half of the buildings are gone, having been razed to keep the business district from looking like a ghost town.

For Parcel Post and Federal Express deliveries, street signs and house numbers were recently installed. There is no longer a Main Street. The street that was clearly Main Street and that everyone called Main Street is now Second Street. Doesn't every town have a Main Street?

Town officials numbered the east/west streets First through Fourth. The street leading into town on the east edge was named East Street—perfect. The street leading into town on the west edge was named Maple Street—not West Street. West Street is two blocks west of East Street in the center of the town. Central Street is between East and West Streets, one block from the east edge of town The final street was named Elm Street. The town has scores of Walnut trees and so they name streets Maple and Elm.

The school is gone, torn down and landscaped to leave no evidence that it ever existed.

The church has closed and the building has been converted to a private residence.

One grain elevator remains, now minus the lumber yard.

The railroad was closed for a period of time. Some lobbying by farm interests restored partial service. The train used to go all of the way to the Mississippi River and then returned the next day. Now the tracks end at the next town four miles west. The tracks were removed beyond the town and some of the roadbed is now farmed. There is no turn- around for the train, so it has to go backward on the return trip.

There is no running to the store now to get a loaf of bread or a quart of milk. You have to go out of town at least four miles.

There is no place for the farmers to "hang out" since the tavern closed.

The petroleum bulk plant that Luke's dad hauled out of is still in use, but in run-down condition. The blacksmith shop was torn down and replaced by a private home.

On the good news side, the pig lot east of town is gone and air quality is up!

The Federal government built a new post office, but there is still no home delivery.

The decline is similar to what happened to many small towns across the country during the past fifty years. There was no way to stop the bleeding.

The first big blow was the closing of the gear plant. It outgrew the post office and its product base grew to the point where more space was needed. The move was to a bigger town about 15 miles away. This eliminated jobs and customers for the tavern, store and automotive garages.

The school consolidated and the high school moved to the neighboring town four miles down the road. This first consolidation was okay, as the grade school fit the school building better without the high school. A second consolidation later involved moving the grade school out of town so the school building was torn down.

First Street

Third Street

The summer baseball and softball leagues folded which made the diamonds unneeded.

The lights, backstops and outfield fences were torn down and another activity was gone for good.

The farmers stopped raising chickens, which eliminated egg production and that resulted in the closing of the egg candling plant. Lack of customers caused the closing of the store. The tavern and restaurant sputtered along under many different managers and finally died.

The church membership dwindled to the point that they could not afford a minister. The population had grown a little, but not as fast as costs. Church attendance was down. People either didn't go to church as much or went out of town. There are no more Christmas church services or potluck dinners in town.

The town does now have garbage pick-up, city water, cable TV and a volunteer fire department with two fire trucks. It is a huge jump from the old telephone office to cell phones. They still have no policeman and just recently the bank was robbed. The robber was caught, though, it was a 17-year old from a neighboring town.

Taking a look back to Luke's jobs. The newspaper circulation is down dramatically from his high of 52 subscribers. The current circulation is 31 and the cost is now $4.30 per week as opposed to 30 cents. Cost could be a factor in the lower circulation, or it could be a reflection on how people now get their news. Many people rely on television or the Internet. Another possibility is that Luke was just one helluva newspaper salesman!

The paper boy no longer has to collect because there is direct billing from the publisher.

There is no cutting weeds out of the beans or corn nor is there any field cultivating. The weeds are controlled by chemicals, which maybe makes their way into the food chain.

Farmers no longer have livestock so hardly anyone bales hay and if they do they are huge bales that are loaded with heavy equipment. Kids learn to play poker now by watching Texas Hold-em on television instead of getting fleeced by the hired men.

The fences are all down and the fields are cultivated right up to the roadside ditch. Hogs are raised in huge confinement sheds, which seems cruel, almost as cruel as getting pounded in the head with a hammer!

The walnut trees have survived, now over a century old, and they still produce a bumper crop of walnuts for the squirrels.

It's a pretty good bet you won't see kids batting rocks anymore.

Epilogue

What happened to Luke? There are many Lukes in the world. They left their small towns and graduated from college and traveled the world. They got jobs and lived their lives in larger communities. Many of them married and had families and adjusted as times changed.

Their kids and grandkids often move to even bigger cities and experience growing up in different cultures with scary challenges and exciting opportunities in a world community that Luke and his friends could never have imagined.

Epilogue II

In this half century plus, there have been countless changes in the world, big and small.

One thing hasn't changed for our country.

We still have war.